JOB
SATISFACTION IN
HIGHER
EDUCATION

TITUS OSHAGBEMI

Order this book online at www.trafford.com
or email orders@trafford.com

Most Trafford titles are also available at major online book retailers.

Printed in the United States of America.

ISBN: 978-1-4669-8954-2 (sc)
ISBN: 978-1-4669-8955-9 (hc)
ISBN: 978-1-4669-8996-2 (e)

Library of Congress Control Number: 2013906581

Trafford rev. 04/18/2013

 www.trafford.com

North America & international
toll-free: 1 888 232 4444 (USA & Canada)
phone: 250 383 6864 ✦ fax: 812 355 4082

Contents

List of Tables

List of Figures

Statement of Aims

This book is about the job satisfaction or dissatisfaction of workers generally, and those in higher education in particular. The aim of the book is to explain how to determine the average level of workers' job satisfaction as a basis for decision and policy making in organisations including the relevant government departments. Future researchers could establish whether in comparison to the current national and fairly comprehensive study, the job satisfaction of workers has improved or worsened over time or the statistics remain similar. If future results show a decline in the levels of workers' job satisfaction, action may be taken by concerned organisational managers to improve this in order to strengthen workers' quality of life. Alternatively, even if empirical results show a good level of workers' job satisfaction, knowledge of the variables responsible for this would help to maintain and not to lessen this level of job satisfaction. In short, a further insight into discussions of worker effectiveness may be gained and worker productivity better understood in relation to their job satisfaction levels. Although research is not conclusive as to whether job satisfaction and productivity are related, if they are, then organisations could benefit from increasing productivity when the job satisfaction levels of their workers are high. Even if job satisfaction and productivity are not related there are humanitarian grounds to support a fairly high level of workers' job satisfaction.

Blurb

This book describes research studies in job satisfaction in higher education, an interesting subject to which many people have contributed articles. The aim of the book is to provide a greater understanding of the overall, as well as some of the more important, determinants of job satisfaction. The book explores the implications of the research findings towards understanding and explaining the level of satisfaction of workers, the implications of these findings towards the effective management of organisations, and speculation on employees' overall productivity. Although data were collected from the United Kingdom for the research described in this book, references were made throughout to the situation in other parts of the world. Containing eleven chapters, the book explains the concept of job satisfaction and its determinants. Its importance is also discussed as well as various models of the construct which are used worldwide, one of which we employed in the investigation of the many aspects of the topic. Four chapters review previous studies on age, rank, length of service, gender and their relationships with job satisfaction. The last chapter reviews related studies on job satisfaction with respect to line managers' supervision, co-workers' behaviour, pay satisfaction, satisfaction with promotions and satisfaction with primary tasks. Before the final summary and conclusions the chapter asks whether the time spent on a task is related to the enjoyment of it, looking at research evidence for the answer.

Preface

Job satisfaction is an interesting subject to which many people have contributed articles. The present book draws on my research studies on job satisfaction in higher education where I have authored several articles in the following journals: *Personnel Review; Education + Training; Reflections on Higher Education; International Journal of Applied Human Resource Management; International Journal of Educational Management; International Journal of Social Economics; International Journal of Sustainability in Higher Education; Women in Management Review; Educational Management and Administration; Employee Relations; Research in Education* and *Managerial Psychology.* I would like to thank the publishers of these journals for permission to draw on some of my articles.

Following on extensive work in this field, coupled to international recognition and awards received for work published on this subject, I have been encouraged to produce a book on job satisfaction for wider dissemination. This book presents the latest findings on the subject for a wider audience of students, teachers and managers. It provides a new approach to the subject, benefiting from different outlooks and includes fresh research on various aspects of job satisfaction.

I share John B. Miner's conviction that the only way to truly advance knowledge in the social sciences is through programmatic research, rather than through research of the so-called *single-shot* variety. To be used effectively programmatic research must, however, be made available in its entirety. This book aims at this objective arising from research studies on job satisfaction. It is to be hoped that the book, in its entirety, is greater than the sum of the individual chapters.

It has been my privilege to be of service and hopefully of benefit to a wide range of students and scholars from Sweden, Germany, the United Kingdom, South Africa, the Philippines, Malaysia, Ghana, Indonesia, Croatia, Thailand, Mexico, Nigeria, the Republic of Ireland, Australia, Turkey and the United States of America. Many of these people have asked for reprints of my papers, enquired about the research instruments used in the study or sought my approval to serve as their advisors in doctoral studies on this subject.

I have discussed ideas on the topic of job satisfaction with colleagues such as David Newman, Brian Webb, and Frances Hill. Charles Hickson and I have jointly written a couple of articles on the subject, while Colin Forde has always cheerfully assisted with statistical analysis. I remain indebted for useful insights gathered from each one of them as indeed from suggestions received from divisional colleagues on the research.

It is my sincere hope that many scholars, especially management, education and psychology scholars, and practicing managers will find the material herein presented both stimulating and helpful. It is also hoped that some of the scholars who approached me for copies of the questionnaire used in the study, and others who have read the findings of this research, will be motivated to conduct similar studies in their countries. Such studies can serve, not only to thoroughly investigate job satisfaction statistics in their own countries, but also for comparative purposes. A follow-up study in the UK could compare the job satisfaction of academics over time. It would indeed be interesting to note whether the job satisfaction of UK academics has increased, decreased or largely remained unchanged, especially in view of recent and current changes in the United Kingdom's higher education system.

The primary aim of this book is to provide a greater understanding of the overall, as well as some of the more important determinants of job satisfaction, or dissatisfaction. The book explores the implications of these research findings towards the effective management of organisations, and towards increasing the level of satisfaction of employees and their overall productivity. The book is about the job satisfaction or dissatisfaction of workers generally, and those in higher education in particular.

One of the aims of the book is to explain how to determine the average level of workers' job satisfaction as a basis for decision and policy making in organizations including the relevant government departments. Future researchers could establish whether in comparison to the current national and fairly comprehensive study, the job satisfaction of workers has improved or worsened over time or the statistics remain similar. If future results show a decline in the levels of workers' job satisfaction, action may be taken by concerned organizational managers to improve this in order to strengthen workers' quality of life. Alternatively, even if empirical results show a good level of workers' job satisfaction, knowledge of the variables responsible for this would help to maintain and not to lessen this level of job satisfaction. In short, a further insight into discussions of worker effectiveness may be gained and worker productivity better understood in relation to their job satisfaction levels. Although research is not conclusive as to whether job satisfaction and productivity are related, if they are, then organizations could benefit from increasing productivity when the job satisfaction levels of their workers are high. Even if job satisfaction and productivity are not related there are humanitarian grounds to support a fairly high level of workers' job satisfaction.

Biography/About the Author

Titus Oshagbemi received his PhD in Management and Administration from the University of Bradford Management Centre (UK) in 1985. He has authored four books and over forty articles on organisational leadership, entrepreneurship, managerial time, job satisfaction and cultural studies. A trained management consultant, the author is active in consultation and development work for public and private sector organisations. A Professor of Management from the University of Jos, Nigeria, he has also taught and researched at The Queen's University of Belfast, United Kingdom. He has visited Canada and more than a dozen States in the USA in addition to a few West African countries.

CHAPTER I

Introduction

THIS CHAPTER EXAMINES THE nature and the sources of job satisfaction and explores its determinants. It discusses the concept of job satisfaction and its importance not only to the individual worker but also to his or her organisation. One way of looking at the importance of job satisfaction is to examine the consequences of job dissatisfaction for the individual and their implications to the organisation. Comments on the theories of job satisfaction and explanations of a popular model of job satisfaction are given.

What is job satisfaction?

Job satisfaction describes how content an individual is with his or her job. It refers to individuals' positive emotional reactions to all the circumstances affecting their jobs. It is an affective reaction to a job that results from a person's comparison of actual outcomes with those that are desired, anticipated or deserved. After decades of research there seems to be a high level of agreement among social scientists on the meaning of the construct. Typically, job satisfaction is conceptualised as a general attitude towards the job. It is this construct, which so many writers have attempted to explain and define, that gives rise to a plethora of definitions.

Locke (1969, p.316; 1976, p.1300)[1] stated that job satisfaction can be viewed as a pleasurable or positive emotional state resulting from the appraisal of one's job or job experience as achieving, or facilitating

---

[1] All references are written in full in the bibliography at the back of the book.

the achievement of one's job values. Locke sees job satisfaction and dissatisfaction to be a function of the perceived relationship between what one wants from one's job and what one perceives it as offering or entailing. Lofquist and Dawis (1969, p.53) noted that satisfaction is "a function of the correspondence between the reinforcer system of the work environment and the individual's needs". Locke and Henne (1986, p.21) wrote that "the achievement of one's job values in the work situation results in the pleasurable emotional state known as job satisfaction". Porter et al. (1975, pp.53-54) characterised satisfaction as a feeling about a job that "is determined by the difference between the amount of some valued outcome that a person receives and the amount of outcome she feels she should receive".

Job satisfaction is therefore a broad term which refers to an individual's general attitude to his or her job. A person with a high level of job satisfaction holds positive attitudes towards the job, whereas a person who is dissatisfied with his or her job holds negative attitudes about it. The term encapsulates the degree to which workers feel their work is satisfying in terms of how secure it is, how useful, how much sense of achievement it brings and how well it is regarded by others. When people speak of employee attitudes, more often than not they mean job satisfaction. In fact the two terms are frequently used synonymously. Attitudes are evaluative statements—either favourable or unfavourable—concerning objects, people or events. They reflect how people feel about something. Similarly, job satisfaction refers to a person's feelings—positive or negative—about his or her job. It is sometimes explained as the difference between the amount of the reward workers receive and the amount they believe they should receive. Anyone who expects little will be easily satisfied. At the same time, the person who expects a great deal and gets it will also be satisfied. However, if one expects a lot but gets little, one will be dissatisfied. The argument is that job satisfaction is a psychological process involving the match between expectations and reality in any individual case. Therefore, as indicated earlier, job satisfaction represents an attitude rather than behaviour, although an individual's behaviour tends to follow from, and is generally consistent with, his or her attitude to a given subject.

As we can see, various definitions result from different conceptualisations of job satisfaction. There is a corresponding variety of publications on the subject and the number grows daily. Locke estimated in 1976, that some 3,350 articles or dissertations had been written on the topic. Cranny *et al.* (1992, p.1), suggested that more than 5000 studies of job satisfaction have been published. Oshagbemi (1996, p.389) suggested that a fresh count of relevant articles and dissertations would double Locke's estimate of only 20 years earlier.

It is sometimes useful to distinguish sources of job satisfaction, because they generally fall into two categories: intrinsic and extrinsic. Intrinsic sources originate from within the individual and have psychological value. Autonomy, which means a degree of independence, such as the ability to choose one's own work pace, is one intrinsic source of satisfaction. In higher education, for example, most academic staff members choose what subject to teach and the topics to research. This gives them intrinsic job satisfaction.

Extrinsic sources of satisfaction originate from outside the individual:—they come from his or her environment. Forces beyond the individual's control determine the frequency and extent of satisfaction. Working conditions, job security, fringe benefits and friendly co-workers are examples of sources of extrinsic satisfaction. Some sources of satisfaction serve a dual purpose in that they can be extrinsic or tangible in nature while having intrinsic or psychological value because of what they symbolise. A high salary and rapid career progress (promotion) would be dual sources of satisfaction to most workers, (i.e. intrinsic as well as extrinsic).

The concept of job satisfaction

Although research into and theorising on the nature, causes and correlates of job satisfaction have mushroomed, the concept remains problematic in terms of a clear and straightforward explanation. Some writers have equated job satisfaction with 'employee attitude' whereas others regard it as 'industrial morale'; the latter term refers to, a group as opposed to an individual phenomenon. The conceptual problem of a precise and unambiguous definition led Katz and Maanem (1976, p.173) to conclude:

> There is perhaps no area in the social sciences fraught with more ambiguity, conflicting opinion or methodological nuance than that of work [job] satisfaction . . . It is indeed a complex, cumbersome and many sided concept for which simple schemes do not exist.

Nevertheless, it is apparent, according to Ejiogu (1980, p.2), that several definitions have a common focus, namely:

> a recognition of the fact that an individual's expression of job satisfaction is an emotional affective personal response as a result of his estimation of the degree to which some fact of job reality is congruent or incongruent with his values.

Cameron (1973, p.1) introduced another dimension to the construct when she said that 'even if a man's job satisfies his needs, he will not express satisfaction with it if he perceives some comparable job as satisfying his needs better or with less effort required'. Thus the notion of equity is to be seen as an important element: it is not simply a matter of need fulfilment. An individual's needs may be fulfilled, but any feeling of satisfaction will still depend on whether he sees his position as comparing satisfactorily with others.

Zaleznik *et al.* (1958, pp.256-257) suggest that a 'total' approach to the question of job satisfaction is desirable, because "the individual's satisfaction or dissatisfaction is determined by his total situation at work and at home, in every aspect of his life". This suggests that job satisfaction is a theoretical concept which is difficult to separate from overall 'life satisfaction'. In this book, job satisfaction is viewed as a unitary rather than a group concept. It is also a concept which can be analysed separately from the life satisfaction of which it is a part (Cranny *et al.* 1992, p.8). Job satisfaction is, in the words of Hoppock (1935, p.47), 'a combination of psychological, physiological and environmental circumstances that causes a person truthfully to say, "I am satisfied with my job". In other words, "people's perceptions of their job satisfaction are related to the value which they place on the various aspects of their job and its environment as sources of satisfaction and dissatisfaction" (Ejiogu, 1980, p.5).

What determines job satisfaction?

As the term implies, work–related variables generally determine job satisfaction, such as the nature of the work, equitable pay and other rewards, supportive colleagues and working conditions. During research into the job satisfaction of university teachers, we incorporated some of these elements in a model of overall job satisfaction. They included the nature of the work (broken down into teaching, research and administration and management), pay, opportunities for promotion, supervision/supervisor's behaviour, colleagues' behaviour and physical conditions/facilities (see Oshagbemi, 1996). Our model of overall job satisfaction closely approximates that of the job descriptive index (JDI) (Smith et al. 1969, 1975, 1985) which is based on five elements: the work itself, pay, promotion, supervision and co-workers. The JDI and its various modifications have been widely used all over the world in job satisfaction studies.

Research suggests that employees tend to prefer a job that gives them opportunities to use their skills and abilities and offers a variety of tasks, freedom to do the job in their own way and feedback on how well they are doing. Workers also want pay systems and promotion policies that they perceive as just, unambiguous and in line with their expectations. Employers and employees are similarly concerned with the work environment for reasons of both personal comfort and job facilitation. They prefer physical surroundings and facilities that are safe, comfortable, clean, and have a minimum of distractions. In addition, for most employees, work also fills the need for social interaction. It is therefore not surprising that friendly and supportive co-workers lead to increased job satisfaction.

It is important, nevertheless, to point out that there are other models and measures of job satisfaction. Cross (1973) suggested that the JDI, as a global measure, may suffer from an American bias. More importantly, a major criticism of the scale is that it was designed to be used across all levels of an organisation whereas the items on the original scale cannot be of equal value to every worker within an organisation. Items suitable for the lower grades of workers are unlikely to be suitable for managers and vice versa. (See the items in the final version of the JDI in Table 1.) To overcome the difficulty of scoring in the original version of the JDI, we quantified levels of satisfaction on each of the dimensions used in our own questionnaire rather than employing the items on the original version. The JDI has largely been validated by several researchers (e.g. Brooke *et al.,* 1988; Roznowski, 1989). Indeed an impressive body of data has been built up to evaluate the JDI and according to Vroom (1964, p.100), it "is without doubt the most carefully constructed measure of job satisfaction in existence".

Table 1: Items in the Final Version of the Job Descriptive Index (JDI)

Each of the five scales was presented on a separate page. The instructions for each scale asked the participant to put Y beside an item if the item described the particular aspect of his or her job (work, pay, etc.), N if the item did not describe that aspect or? if he or she could not decide. The response shown beside each item is the one scored in the "satisfied" direction for each scale.

Work

Y Fascinating

N Satisfying

N Boring

Y Good

Y Creative

Y Respected

N Hot

Y Pleasant

Y Useful

N Tiresome

Y Healthful

Y Challenging

N On your feet

N Frustrating

N Simple

N Endless

Y Gives sense of accomplishment

Supervision

Y Asks my advice

N Hard to please

N Impolite

Y Praises good work

Y Tactful

Y Influential

Y Up-to-date

N Doesn't supervise enough

N Quick tempered

Y Tells me where I stand

N Annoying

N Stubborn

Y Knows job well

N Bad

Pay

Y Income adequate for normal expenses

Y Satisfactory profit sharing

N Barely live on income

N Bad

N Income provides luxuries

N Insecure

N Less than I deserve

Y Highly paid

N Underpaid

Promotions

Y Good opportunity for advancement

N Opportunity somewhat limited

Y Promotion on ability

N Dead-end job

Y Good chance for promotion

N Unfair promotion policy

N Infrequent promotions

Y Regular promotions

Y Fairly good chance of promotion

Co-workers

Y Stimulating

N Boring

N Slow

Y Ambitious

N Stupid

Y Responsible

Y Fast

Y Intelligent

N Easy to make enemies

N Talk too much

Y Smart

N Lazy

N Unpleasant

N No privacy

Y Intelligent	Y Active
Y Leaves me on my own	N Narrow interests
N Lazy	Y Loyal
Y Around when needed	N Hard to meet

Source: Smith *et al.* (1985), *The Revised Job Descriptive Index,* Chicago, Rand McNally, p.83.

In his own formulation, Cross (1973) introduced the firm as a whole to the five facets measured by the JDI. He stated that employee attitudes towards the organisation and its policies had been identified as a separate grouping by several researchers (Kahn, 1960; Harrison, 1961). Cross came up with six facets instead of the five proposed by the JDI. Soutar and Weaver (1982) and Bell and Weaver (1987) have carried out separate studies which largely validate the instrument proposed by Cross.

It should also be pointed out that the Minnesota Satisfaction Questionnaire (Weiss et al., 1967) is one of the most widely encountered in the literature and has been widely validated time and time again. There are short (25 items) and long (100 items) versions of the questionnaire. The short form is simpler to complete, but provides less information, whereas the long form would yield more data but takes considerably longer to complete.

The question of what determines job satisfaction is, therefore, not unrelated to measures of job satisfaction, because each measure attempts to capture the essence of the concept. Although there are several measures for collecting data regarding job satisfaction, we limited our research to, perhaps, the most popular one—questionnaires using Likert scales—which allowed seven responses with the highest and lowest score indicating extreme degrees of either agreement or disagreement, and with the middle score showing neutrality.

The importance of job satisfaction

From the sheer number of publications on job satisfaction we know that the topic is important to many people. It is important because of its relevance to the physical and mental well being of employees; it has relevance to human health. Work is an important aspect of people's lives and most people spend a large proportion of their time at work. An understanding of the factors involved in job satisfaction is relevant to improving the well being of a significant number of people. Although the pursuit of increased satisfaction is essentially of humanitarian value, Smith and others stated that "trite as it may seem, satisfaction is a legitimate goal in itself" (Smith et al. 1969, p.3); in addition to its humanitarian value, job satisfaction seems to be extensively researched in a variety of organisations for work-related objectives. This is because of the implicit assumptions that job satisfaction is a potential determinant of productivity, absenteeism, turnover, in-role job performance and extra-role behaviour, and that management has the ability to influence the primary antecedents of job attitudes.

Job satisfaction is exceedingly important not only for the well being of individual workers but also for the organisation. Low levels of job satisfaction have been related to early retirement and such problems as turnover, absenteeism, union activity, tardiness, grievances and hostile activity. These problems can be costly and disruptive to the smooth running of an organisation.

Job satisfaction can play an important role in the ability of an organisation to attract and retain qualified workers. For example, an organisation that is known for not treating its workers particularly well will experience problems in this respect. Thus, there are economic reasons for organisations to want their employees to be satisfied with their jobs. An organisation that has satisfied and capable workers may spend less on recruiting and training new workers. Palmore (1969) suggested that highly satisfied workers have better physical and mental health records and therefore live longer.

It should be pointed out, however, that the evidence is strictly based on correlation analyses, and causation should not be presumed automatically. Perhaps other factors such as income and educational level could be largely responsible for the observed correlation. However, serious job dissatisfaction often leads to stress, which in turn can result in physiological disorders such as ulcers.

Perhaps the most important reason for governments and employers attending to workers' satisfaction is a moral one. Given that most people must work in order to earn a living and most people spend most of their adult lives at work, it can be argued that employers have a moral obligation to make the work experience personally rewarding or, at least, employers should preserve human dignity at work. It should be seen as one of the social responsibilities of any organisation, public or private.

The importance of job satisfaction can also be looked at from the consequences of job dissatisfaction, which generally leads to withdrawal behaviour on the part of the workers who are dissatisfied. People tend to withdraw from situations that are painful or unrewarding. The principle of reward and punishment helps to explain employee behaviour in relation to their level of job dissatisfaction. Studies of absenteeism in the USA have often found that less satisfied workers are more likely to be absent from work (Hackett and Guion, 1985). It is interesting to observe that more work time is lost, each year, from absenteeism than from strikes and lockouts. It is also generally believed that poor timekeeping tends to reflect employee dissatisfaction among other factors (Adler and Golan, 1981).

Studies have shown, with a fair degree of consistency, that dissatisfied workers are more likely to quit their jobs than satisfied ones. There are, of course, other reasons for workers to resign other than lack of satisfaction. What is important is that job dissatisfaction is often an important factor (Carsten and Spector, 1987). There are studies to suggest that it leads to early retirement (Hanisch and Hulin, 1990) and speculations abound that lower-level jobs (job level) sometimes lead workers to retire early. Some studies have also suggested that increased union activity has long been accepted as a consequence of employee dissatisfaction (Hammer and Smith, 1978).

Finally there is good reason to believe that extremely dissatisfied workers are sometimes involved in hostile actions against their employers or co-workers, such as theft, openly criticising the employer to customers or the public, sabotaging machinery or vandalising company property. Dissatisfied workers may also introduce computer viruses as a form of revenge. Employers and employees alike are reluctant to discuss the matter, so there has been little empirical research on it to date.

Theories/ Models of job satisfaction

Although 'theories of job satisfaction' are mentioned in the titles of many publications, perusal invariably reveals discussion of motivation theories (Wahi, 1978; Ejiogu, 1980), variance theory or the job characteristics model (Hackman and Oldham, 1975; Fincham and Rhodes, 1999, p.146-153). Job satisfaction is not the same as motivation, although it is clearly linked. There are no 'theories' of job satisfaction as such but several theories of motivation abound. Unfortunately, some sources discuss motivation theories as theories of job satisfaction and this adds to the confusion. All we have is a popular concept useful to explain and measure the main parameters involved when there is a reduction or an increase in an individual's level of job satisfaction. This is the JDI proposed by Smith et al. (1969, 1975, 1985), for ascertaining an individual's overall level. The JDI is often modified in practice when researchers want to study the level of job satisfaction among specific occupational groups. It is the summation of the five elements in the JDI that attempts to estimate overall job satisfaction of any occupational group. Conceptually, satisfaction with any of these five aspects of job satisfaction contributes to overall job satisfaction.

One of the biggest preludes to the study of job satisfaction was the Hawthorne studies. These studies (1924-1933), primarily credited to Elton Mayo (1947) of the Harvard Business School, sought to find the effects of various conditions (most notably illumination) on workers' productivity. These studies ultimately showed that novel changes in work conditions temporarily increase productivity:—this is called the Hawthorne Effect. It was later found that this increase resulted, not from the new conditions, but from the knowledge of being observed. This finding provided strong evidence that people work for purposes other than pay, which paved the way for researchers to investigate other factors in job satisfaction.

Scientific management (otherwise known as Taylorism) also had a significant impact on the study of job satisfaction. Frederick Winslow Taylor's book, *Principles of Scientific Management* (1947), argued that there was a single best way to perform any given work task. This book contributed to a change in industrial production philosophies, causing a shift from skilled labour and piecework towards the more modern approach of assembly lines and hourly wages. The initial use of scientific management by industries greatly increased productivity because workers were forced to work at a faster pace. However, workers became exhausted and dissatisfied, thus leaving researchers with new questions to answer regarding job satisfaction. Some argue that Maslow's hierarchy of needs theory (1954), a motivation theory, laid the foundation for job satisfaction theory. This theory explains that people seek to satisfy five specific needs in life:—physiological needs, safety needs, social needs, self-esteem needs, and self-actualization. This model served as a good basis from which early researchers could develop job satisfaction theories.

Edwin Locke's Range of Affect or Goal-Setting Theory (1976) is arguably the most famous job satisfaction model. The main premise of this theory is that satisfaction is determined by a discrepancy between what one wants in a job and what one has in a job. Further, the theory states that how much one values a given facet of work (e.g. the degree of autonomy in a position) moderates how satisfied/ dissatisfied one becomes when expectations are/are not met. When a person values a particular facet of a job, his or her satisfaction is more greatly impacted both positively (when expectations are met) and negatively (when expectations are not met), compared with one who does not value that facet. To illustrate, if Employee A values autonomy in the workplace and Employee B is indifferent about autonomy, then Employee A would be more satisfied in a position that offers a high degree of autonomy and less satisfied in a position with little or no autonomy compared with Employee B. This theory also states that too much of a particular facet will produce stronger feelings of satisfaction the more a worker values that facet.

Another well-known job satisfaction theory is the Dispositional Theory. It is a very general theory that suggests that people have innate dispositions that cause them to have tendencies toward a certain level of satisfaction, regardless of their job. This approach became a notable explanation of job satisfaction in light of evidence that job satisfaction tends to be stable over time and across careers and jobs. A significant model that narrowed the scope of Dispositional Theory was the Core-Evaluations Model, proposed by Timothy Judge and his colleagues. Judge (1998) and others argued that there are four core self-evaluations that determine one's disposition towards job satisfaction: self-esteem, general self-efficacy, locus of control, and neuroticism. This model states that higher levels of self-esteem (the value one places on one self) and general self-efficacy (the belief in one's own competence) lead to higher work satisfaction. Having an internal locus of control, believing one has control over one's own life, as opposed to outside forces having control, leads to higher job satisfaction. Finally, lower levels of neuroticism (the tendency to have negative emotions) lead to higher job satisfaction.

Frederick Herzberg's two-factor theory (1959)—otherwise known as Motivator-Hygiene Theory,—although typically thought of as a motivation theory that explains job satisfaction, states that satisfaction and dissatisfaction are driven by different factors:—motivation and hygiene. Motivators are aspects of the job that make people want to perform and provide people with satisfaction. Hygiene refers to the aspects of a job that do not make people satisfied (such as pay), but their absence would cause dissatisfaction.

Needless to state there are several other theories of motivation such as David McClelland's Achievement motivation-need theory (1967), Victor Vroom's Expectancy theory (1964), Stacy Adams' Equity theory (1965), B F Skinner's Reinforcement theory (1974), Douglas McGregor's theory X and Y (1960), Clayton Alderfer's Existence, Relatedness and Growth theory (1972), and so on. Apart from acknowledging their existence and importance, the intention is not to review these theories in this book because it is felt that they are not directly applicable to determining the job satisfaction of workers. However, they may be useful in estimating the motivational level of workers towards the performance of their jobs. Whereas content theories attempt to define what motivates individuals, process theories outline the variables affecting motivation but they are not prescriptive.

In this book, therefore, we have been careful not to discuss motivation theories and label them 'job satisfaction theories'. As people are looking for different things from their work, it is understandable that some jobs may be satisfying to some and not to others. Following Smith et al. (1969, 1975, 1985), however, it can be asserted that a general theory of overall job satisfaction will be concerned primarily with five variables, namely: satisfaction with, the work itself, pay, promotion, supervision and co-workers. Within higher education, Oshagbemi (1996) suggested that overall job satisfaction is a function of eight variables, satisfaction with: teaching, research, administration and management, pay, promotions, co-workers, supervision/ supervisory behaviour, and physical conditions/working facilities.

Structure of the book

An introduction to the topic of job satisfaction has been given in this chapter. Chapter 2 presents the background to the research which underpins the book. It discusses the justifications for the study, the method and measurement, responses to the survey and the background of the respondents. Chapter 3 describes the overall picture of job satisfaction and in particular it highlights the satisfaction of the participants with their primary duties and with the other aspects of their job. The chapter also looks at the issue of measuring or determining the level of job satisfaction in practice. It presents and discusses general as well as specific measures of job satisfaction and attempts to evaluate these measures by comparing their advantages and disadvantages. Chapter 4 discusses factors which contribute to satisfaction and dissatisfaction within the context of the two-factor theory and the situational occurrences theory of job satisfaction.

Chapter 5 looks at a classification of university teachers in to three job satisfaction profiles: happy workers, satisfied workers, unhappy workers. It compares the three groups of university teachers especially in relation to their primary functions and other aspects of their job. It also explores the implications of the groupings. Chapter 6 reports on a comparative study of academics and their managers identifying similarities and differences in their job satisfaction levels after reviewing the relevant literature. Chapters 7 to 10 review previous studies on age, rank, length of service, gender and job satisfaction respectively. They also present and discuss our own empirical findings in these interesting areas of the literature on job satisfaction.

Job satisfaction is a very wide subject and research area. In Chapter 11, related studies are looked at briefly. These include job satisfaction with respect to line managers' supervision, co-workers' behaviour, pay satisfaction, satisfaction with promotions, and satisfaction with primary tasks. Before the final summary and conclusions the chapter also asks whether the time spent on a task is related to the enjoyment of it, looking at research evidence for the answer.

CHAPTER 2

Background to the Research

Introduction

THIS CHAPTER PRESENTS THE background to the research, justification for the study and the basic method used to gather data. Responses to the study as well as the background of respondents are also detailed. However, as would be expected, discussions in the book are wide ranging and they include opinions and issues, including those outside the UK, which are of relevance to higher education generally.

This research arose from the concern of the researcher, himself an academic, about the realities of job satisfaction among academics in UK universities. Anecdotal evidence suggested that, in comparison to the past, the level of job satisfaction was low. There was a clear need to establish the current position to provide future studies with a comparison of statistics, then and now, so as to determine whether, in fact, job satisfaction has increased, decreased or largely remained unchanged.

The study also examined the job satisfaction of university teachers with a view to understanding certain determinants, their relationship to certain variables, and their implications for effective academic management. The objectives of the study included a survey of job satisfaction levels of university teachers, and the examination of the relationships, if any, between age, gender, length of service, job seniority and job satisfaction. The study also examined the opinions and perceptions of teachers on those factors relevant to improving job satisfaction levels and discussed the relevance of the topic to the subject of academic management in UK universities.

This chapter discusses the justification for the study, outlines its method and measurement and provides a summary of the responses to the survey indicating sample and percentage responses.

Before carrying out the primary survey, a pilot study was conducted within two universities. The results of the pilot study and comments from colleagues on the adequacy of the questionnaire were useful in making certain changes to the research instrument used in the national survey. Finally, the background of respondents participating in the study—their age, rank, gender and length of service (in present university and in higher education)—will be highlighted. The respondents' areas of academic discipline and their leadership or management responsibility are also discussed.

Justification for the study

Job satisfaction is one of the most researched topics in management and organisational psychology, and thousands of articles and dissertations have been written on the subject. Despite this volume of work and many publications on job satisfaction, Guion stated that several issues remain to be addressed on the subject. Attempting to address some of the issues would require, according to Guion, an agenda for more articles and more books (Cranny et al., 1992, p.279)! Many scholars have stated that there can be no question of job satisfaction studies being viewed as a stagnant area relying merely on past research, but rather that job satisfaction studies continue to be a vital and growing area of research with ties to other concepts and interests. This is clearly associated with the complexity and variety of issues normally having a bearing on job satisfaction, its components and its correlates.

There are three main justifications for undertaking studies on the job satisfaction of university teachers. Firstly, university teachers seem to differ from other occupational groups in certain important respects. A sound knowledge of this work group may add significant insights into our understanding of the total picture of the job satisfaction of workers in general. Indeed, academics and their managers all over the world are a unique and interesting group worthy of detailed studies. Their primary jobs are in teaching, research and administration and management. Few other groups of workers perform such a disparate array of functions. A further characteristic of university teachers is that, by and large, they have considerable control over their jobs—what to teach and, within increasing constraints, what topics to research (Oshagbemi, 1996).

In addition, acceptance of leadership responsibility tends to be voluntary within academia. These characteristics are generally different from the situation in industry or government. In the latter situations, managers tend to perform tasks within a limited range of discretion rather than determining the nature of their tasks in the first instance. To enhance the development of comprehensive theories of job satisfaction, various dimensions of job satisfaction in different work situations need to be investigated and understood. The effective management of particular groups, such as university teachers, calls for information on their job satisfaction, the causes, the patterns and the consequences, among other considerations.

Secondly, it is mostly university teachers who conduct investigations into the job satisfaction levels of other occupational groups. It is timely, therefore, that university teachers themselves should be a focus of studies on job satisfaction.

A survey of relevant literature gives a list of past studies, ranging from the job satisfaction of Canadian physicians (Richardson and Burke, 1991) to the job satisfaction of ethnic minorities in the Netherlands (Verkuyten et al., 1993), or the job satisfaction of accountants in Singapore (Goh *et al.,* 1991). Job satisfaction studies have been published on librarians, police officers, soldiers, nurses, paramedics, salesmen and sales executives, school principals, dentists, engineers, journalists, casino card–dealers, and several other groups of subjects but, surprisingly, few studies that focus on university teachers have been reported. Yet, the majority of published studies have been conducted by university teachers. Clearly further studies on the job satisfaction of university teachers are not only justified, but long overdue. Gruneberg and Startup (1978, p.75), state that 'academics are an interesting and in many ways atypical group of people'. They are therefore worthy of further investigation, into their job satisfaction and other criteria.

Thirdly, a further justification for undertaking studies into the job satisfaction of university teachers, especially in the UK, stems from recent and current changes occurring in higher education. As Eggins (1994) and Davies (1994) point out, these changes include the growth of mature student entry, the expansion of courses in the sciences, the removal of the binary divide, the reduction in student grants, and the likelihood that students will increasingly have to pay more for their education. Some of these changes have arisen from pressures of demand, the cultural shift in the way in which higher education is viewed, financial pressures, structural and managerial diversity and the diversity of university missions or emphases.

One can speculate that some of these changes have affected the job satisfaction or dissatisfaction of university teachers. This book is aimed at providing a greater understanding of the overall job satisfaction or dissatisfaction of university teachers, as well as some of the more important determinants, and it explores the implications of these research findings towards the effective management of universities.

There is also a strong theoretical justification for the research leading to this book. There is a gap in knowledge on job satisfaction pertaining to university teachers as evidenced when the author conducted a preliminary review of the database held by the Institute of Scientific Information for relevant publications on job satisfaction.

Using the Social Sciences Citation Index on 'job satisfaction' between 1981 and 1993, there were as many as 744 publications recorded in the 13 years for which data were available. When the search focused on studies of job satisfaction where teachers were the subjects, less than five per cent of the 744 publications dealt with the job satisfaction of teachers (Oshagbemi, 1995, p.65). The review at this stage included all teachers—primary and secondary teachers as well as teachers in tertiary institutions all over the world. When job satisfaction studies relating to university teachers in Britain were specifically sought, the Institute of Scientific Information Social Sciences Database revealed none between 1981 and 1993. From 1994 untill now, however, increasing numbers of publications on job satisfaction of academics were recorded although the numbers were still very low.

A few job-satisfaction related studies, with university teachers as subjects were reported before 1981. The studies identified include those conducted by Nicholson and Miljus (1972), Gruneburg et al., (1974a, 1974b), and Gruneberg and Startup (1978). These studies discussed the effect of geographical factors on the job satisfaction of university teachers, the job satisfaction and turnover among liberal arts college professors, the job satisfaction of university teachers and the university teachers' satisfaction with promotional procedures.

It is important to note that the majority of these relevant studies were published more than 30 years ago. In addition, without exception, each of the studies was carried out within only one university system. A common problem with these studies is therefore the difficulty of generalising the findings because they were basically case studies of the situation in specific universities. Thirty years also dates these studies because numerous university practices and policies affecting the job satisfaction of teachers have since been introduced or have been significantly modified over the years. This review has therefore shown a justification for the research, which underlies the contents of this book. It reveals that despite thousands of publications on job satisfaction generally, there was not a single comprehensive job-satisfaction study on UK university teachers not only for the 13 years between 1981 and 1993 but also largely since that time. It must be pointed out that this review does not concern itself with specific job satisfaction studies such as age–job satisfaction studies or gender–job satisfaction studies or studies of specific facets of job satisfaction such as pay satisfaction or promotional satisfaction per se. This review does however consider all comprehensive job satisfaction studies involving university teachers as subjects.

Method and measurement

The research method employed in the study leading to this book was a questionnaire survey. In spite of limitations in the use of questionnaires to measure attitudes, Halsey and Trow (1971) and especially Gruneberg (1979, p.4) summarised the consensus opinion that unfortunately, 'there are few, if any, alternatives which can give the same kind of information as questionnaires, as quickly or as economically'. For example, interviews to assess attitudes are more time consuming, more expensive and they are not free from any bias which may be introduced by the interviewer. The use of questionnaires was therefore adopted, not as an infallible means of measuring job satisfaction, but rather, 'as instruments for approximating the truth'.

To measure job satisfaction, a slightly modified version of the job descriptive index (JDI) was used (Smith et al., 1969, 1975, 1985). The JDI employs five scales designed to measure satisfaction, namely, nature of work, present pay, opportunities for promotion, supervision and co-workers. The summation of the five scales gives a measure of overall job satisfaction. The JDI is one of the most popular measures of job satisfaction and has been found to produce reliable results (Imparato, 1972).

1. teaching,
2. research,

3. administration and management,
4. present pay,
5. promotion,
6. co-workers,
7. supervision and
8. working conditions/physical facilities.

The total of the eight scales gives a summary measure of overall job satisfaction.

The markings used ranged from 1 to 7 representing, 1 = 'Extremely dissatisfied', 2 = 'Very dissatisfied', 3 = 'Dissatisfied', 4 = 'Indifferent', 5 = 'Satisfied', 6 = 'Very satisfied', 7 = 'Extremely satisfied'. The criteria were equally weighted in computing overall job satisfaction.

The job elements in the study are consistent with findings on the measurement of job satisfaction (Wanous and Lawler, 1972; Giles and Field, 1978; Schneider and Dachler, 1978; Kulik et al., 1988; Scapello and Campbell, 1983; Loher et al., 1985). Some demographic questions were introduced in the questionnaire requesting respondents to indicate age, gender, length of service in present university and in higher education, academic rank leadership and discipline.

The objectives of the study included an examination of the opinions and perceptions of teachers on factors relevant to improving their job satisfaction. Section B of the questionnaire requested subjects to rate the importance of certain factors believed to affect satisfaction or dissatisfaction. Part of Section B attempted to identify the importance of some items, believed to affect job satisfaction, on a scale. Thus, on prospects for promotion, for example, it was aimed at not only finding out the satisfaction on this aspect of the position, but also whether it is the criteria, the procedure, or the subjectivity in the application of the criteria that university teachers are more, or less, dissatisfied with. Section C of the questionnaire, was initially developed by Nicholson and Miljus (1972) for a survey of a college faculty in a university. It was later modified and used by Giles and

Field (1978) on another sample of university teachers. This study includes a further modification of the version used by Giles and Field. A copy of the questionnaire is given in the Appendix.

Responses to the survey

In administering the questionnaire, a sample of universities, including older and newer ones, was chosen. All respondents were guaranteed confidentiality. Anonymity was not promised because it was thought that if the response rate was low there might be the need to follow up with reminder letters urging respondents who were yet to return their completed questionnaires to do so. As it turned out the response rate was quite satisfactory. Information about the university teachers was obtained from the Commonwealth Universities Yearbook. This source contains the list of all UK universities and their teachers arranged according to departments and academic ranks. A total of 1,102 questionnaires were sent to potential respondents chosen from 23 universities in the UK. To increase the response rate, the researcher enclosed a stamped addressed envelope for the return of each questionnaire.

Initially there was a response of 554 completed questionnaires, and an additional 12 questionnaires were returned after the first analysis had begun, giving a total of 566 university teachers who returned usable questionnaires. This represents a 51.4 per cent response rate from the randomly selected sample. Potential respondents were only contacted once. Completed and usable questionnaires were received from all four regions of the U K, namely, England, Wales, Scotland and N. Ireland.

Background of the respondents

Table 2 gives a breakdown of the university teachers who responded to the questionnaire. The Table shows the distribution of respondents' age, gender, rank, length of service in present university and in higher education, areas of academic discipline, and their leadership or management responsibilities.

Table 2: Background of respondents

	Percentage
Age (years)	
< 35	14.3
35–44	35.0
45–54	36.7
55+	14.0
	100.0
Rank	
Lecturer	54.9
Senior Lecturer	31.2
Reader	4.3
Professor	8.5
Other	1.1
	100.0
Gender	
Male	60.8
Female	39.2
	100.0
Length of service in higher education (years)	
0–5	14.9
6–10	21.0
11–20	32.3
21–30	25.9
31+	5.9
	100.0
Length of service in present university (years)	
0–5	28.5
6–10	20.8
11–20	27.1
21–30	20.2
31+	3.4
	100.0

Area of academic discipline

Medicine/pharmacy/dentistry/nursing	11.9
Engineering/computing/architecture/archaeology/ building	17.9
Arts/law/education	23.3
Social sciences/management/accountancy	21.7
Natural sciences/agriculture/mathematics	23.9
Others	1.3
	100.0

Leadership or management responsibility

Head, director, dean, provost, etc.	12.2
Not currently in charge of an academic unit or group	61.3
Holding other management posts	26.5
	100.0

The information in Table 2 shows the academic background of respondents was very wide and covered most subject areas in the universities. The distribution of the length of service spent in higher education shows that respondents ranged from relative newcomers who had spent less than five years (about 15% to workers who had spent more than 30 years in the university system (about 6%). As would be expected, a large percentage of workers (almost 80%) fall between the newcomers and the workers with service over a much longer period.

Almost 30 per cent of respondents had worked for less than 5 years in their present universities. This percentage is about twice the corresponding percentage of respondents who had worked in higher education during the same period. The comparison suggests some rates of staff turnover, retirement, or new recruitment necessitated perhaps because of an expansion of universities, which makes about one-third of academic staff relatively new in their present institutions. In fact, almost 50 per cent of the respondents had worked for ten years or less in their present universities. The corresponding figure for those who had worked in higher education during the same period is 36 per cent. It is possible that these figures compare favourably with similar figures of the length of service of workers within other employment sectors, especially workers within other public sector organisations. Unfortunately, although *Social Trends,* a yearly publication of the Government Statistical Service, contains statistics on the usual hours worked by people in full-time and part-time employment, the average length of service which people put into their working lives is not reported (Church, 1994).

Table 2 shows that the majority of the respondents were lecturers (about 55%) and a significant percentage were of senior lecturer rank. The relatively few readers and professors seem to be representative of the percentage of these top officers in the academic population. Some 39 per cent of respondents were female. However, considering the estimated proportion of females in the total population, the percentage of those who responded to our questionnaire can certainly not be considered low.

It was noted from the data analyses, that only one respondent was less than 25 years of age. It is however not clear whether this finding suggests an ageing academic population or whether the average age of academics tends to be slightly higher than the average age of workers in other employment sectors. It was further observed that the percentage of respondents who were less than 35 years old was about the same percentage of those who were older than 55 years. Over 70 per cent of respondents were in the 35-54 year age bracket.

About 12 per cent of respondents held managerial posts as head of department or division, director of school, dean of faculty, provost or head of a unit, (e.g. an institute or centre). The percentage of those who held other management posts, such as year tutor, chairperson of a research group, project co-ordinator, director of undergraduate programmes, was about double this figure of 12 per cent. Clearly, the majority of the respondents were not currently in charge of an academic unit or group. However, it does not follow that this group did not have some administrative assignments, at least on an occasional, if not, on a regular basis.

CHAPTER 3

Job Satisfaction: An Overview and Measurement

Introduction

THIS CHAPTER CONTAINS 2 parts. The first part presents an overview of the general findings of the research programme described in Chapter 2, which collected information on the extent to which university teachers were satisfied with their jobs. The information indicates that levels of satisfaction are greatest with regard to the core role of teaching and to a lesser extent with research. Considerable dissatisfaction was found with regard to salary levels and promotional prospects. The second part discusses the measurement of the concept of job satisfaction, with an empirical study and consequent recommendations. This part of the chapter observes that managers interested in finding out overall job satisfaction levels of their workers often face the problem of the appropriate measure of job satisfaction to adopt: single versus multiple-item? It compares results of a single versus a multiple-item measure employed to investigate the job satisfaction of university teachers. The purpose of the study was to ascertain the superiority or otherwise of measures used in ascertaining the overall job satisfaction of workers. The outcome of the study shows that the single-item measure overestimated the percentage of people satisfied with their jobs and grossly underestimated both the percentage of workers who were dissatisfied and those that showed indifference, in comparison to the figures from the multiple-item measure. The conclusion is that results from a single-item measure tend to paint a picture of job satisfaction that is rosier, than the results conveyed by a multiple-item measure would justify.

The overall picture

The first part of this chapter presents and discusses the results of the questionnaire survey. A breakdown of the respondents' level of satisfaction or dissatisfaction with aspects of their jobs is provided in Tables 3 and 4. Table 3 presents the average ratings and the variability of these ratings, and Table 4 shows the percentages of respondents who were satisfied, dissatisfied, or indifferent to various aspects of their jobs.

Table 3: Average ratings of respondents on the satisfaction or dissatisfaction derived from aspects of their jobs

Aspect of job	Mean score	Modal score	Median score	Standard deviation
Teaching	5.09	5	5	1.20
Research	4.66	5	5	1.58
Administration and management	3.93	5	4	1.40
Present pay	3.44	3	3	1.46
Promotions	3.44	3	3	1.50
Head of unit's supervision/ behaviour	4.18	5	5	1.73
Co-workers' behaviour	4.81	5	5	1.23
Physical conditions/working facilities	4.33	5	5	1.51

A finding from these tables is that the respondents' ratings of satisfaction derived from teaching, research, and their colleagues' behaviour were high. These positive ratings are clearly shown in the percentages of the respondents who were satisfied with those aspects of their jobs, a figure ranging from some 65 to 80 per cent. It is useful to note that the variability of the responses was particularly low on teaching and on interaction with colleagues. This indicates a consistent and a re-assuring positive response from university teachers on these aspects of their jobs.

Ratings by respondents on the satisfaction derived from their head of unit's behaviour, as well on physical conditions and working facilities in their universities, were rather lower. However, more than 50 per cent of respondents were satisfied with each of these aspects of their jobs. There is a rather wide variability in the respondents' ratings of these aspects, especially with the rating on satisfaction derived from the head of unit's behaviour. This indicates that, in the case of satisfaction derived from the head of unit's supervision, some respondents were 'very satisfied' with their head's behaviour, but a significant number were 'seriously dissatisfied'.

Table 4: Percentages of respondents who were satisfied, dissatisfied or indifferent to aspects of their jobs

Aspect of job	*Satisfied*★ %	*Dissatisfied*★★ %	*Indifferent* %
Teaching	79.5	12.8	7.7
Research	64.8	26.6	8.6
Administration and management	40.2	36.8	23.0
Present pay	29.9	54.3	15.8
Promotions	26.4	50.1	23.5
Head of unit's supervision/ behaviour	52.4	34.3	13.3
Co-workers' behaviour	69.7	17.0	13.3
Physical conditions/working facilities	56.9	30.9	12.2

★ Incorporating respondents who were satisfied, very satisfied and extremely satisfied.

★★ Incorporating respondents who were dissatisfied, very dissatisfied and extremely dissatisfied.

This situation suggests that some management training to assist academic managers in the performance of their tasks is required, and that the selection/appointment of academic managers should be based, not only on research competence, but also on some measure of managerial capability. For greater effectiveness, universities should focus on both the selection and training of their academic managers.

The mean ratings of satisfaction derived from the university teachers' administrative and managerial functions, their present pay, and their promotions were low. Mean ratings of less than four were obtained in each of these three considerations and these ratings, in fact, suggest dissatisfaction with these aspects of their jobs. University teachers' dissatisfaction with promotion and present salaries was serious, with mode and median ratings of only three in each of these two aspects of their jobs. The interpretation from these statistics is that the majority of respondents were clearly dissatisfied with these aspects of their jobs.

Table 4 shows that less than 30 per cent of respondents were satisfied with their promotions and only some 30 per cent were satisfied with their present pay. However, more than 50 per cent of respondents were dissatisfied with both their present pay and their promotion (see Table 4). A significant proportion of approximately one out of four academics was 'indifferent' to their promotional prospects. This group may well represent readers and senior lecturers who have reached the top of their salary scale.

The overall feelings of respondents are difficult to summarise in terms of the survey results. Respondents seem to be 'very satisfied' with their main tasks, teaching and research, but they were clearly dissatisfied with some aspects of their jobs. A moderately high level of job satisfaction by university teachers may, in general, represent the feelings of most workers (Oshagbemi, 1996).

Satisfaction with primary duties

The primary duties of university teachers are teaching, research, and administration and management. The satisfaction derived by respondents from these aspects is now considered in greater detail.

Figures in Tables 3 and 4 show clearly that teaching contributes more to the university teachers' satisfaction than research, which, in turn, contributes more to overall satisfaction than administration and management. The differences between the satisfactions derived from teaching and the satisfaction derived from research is statistically significant at the $p<0.001$ level, and the differences between the satisfaction derived from research and from administration and management is also statistically significant at the $p<0.001$ level (t–test).

These results are consistent with earlier findings by Gruneberg and Startup that 'teaching is a more satisfying aspect of the university's life than is research' (1978, p.76). From the list of factors contributing to satisfaction or dissatisfaction, respondents seem to largely enjoy the courses they teach, and most staff members seem to choose the content of their courses. However, some teachers expressed dissatisfaction with class size and their teaching load. In the traditional universities, however, the importance of research tends to overshadow the importance of teaching. It is important to observe the relatively high standard deviation on satisfaction with research (Table 3). This suggests considerable variation among academics in their levels of competence and confidence in research.

Where teaching is related to research, it is clear that teachers tend to be more satisfied with both teaching and research. Unfortunately, as Halsey and Trow found from their own study, academics who were primarily oriented towards teaching rated their promotion chances lower than those primarily oriented towards research (1971, p.337-341). Thus, although there may be intrinsic gains from teaching, intrinsic gains and extrinsic rewards seem to flow more from research.

With the current changes in university policies, however, research as well as teaching will now both be assessed in most universities in the UK. In some research assessment exercises, some universities chose not to take part referring to themselves as specialising in undergraduate teaching only. It is not clear if the State will allow 'teaching only' universities, a term which some commentators have referred to as contradictory. It is perhaps debatable whether university education can really occur and flourish in an atmosphere devoid of enquiry and research.

In research, an area where university teachers have expressed dissatisfaction is the emphasis often given to quantity instead of the quality of publications. The government seems to be responding to this concern. Compared to the first three research assessment exercises (1986, 1989, 1992), in the fourth (1996) and the fifth exercises (2001), only a limited number of publications were assessed per member of the academic staff as a basis for estimating the research rating of academic units. This trend is likely to continue in the future to encourage high quality publications.

In contrast to teaching and research, where a high level of satisfaction was generally expressed, university teachers were dissatisfied with administrative activities. Many respondents complained that excessive paperwork was demanded of them and that time spent on administrative duties reduced the time remaining, especially for research. Some academic staff detested the nature of some of their administrative obligations. In the words of one of the respondents, 'the government has commercialised university education'.

The dissatisfaction which university teachers found with administrative and managerial duties stems, perhaps, from the belief of some that administration and management, notwithstanding the relatively high proportion of time spent on those duties, were not really their primary functions. In an earlier study by Oshagbemi (1988), a sample of British academic managers indicated that, compared to research, administrative duties did not constitute a core obligation. Moreover, the academic managers enjoyed doing research in preference to administration and management (Oshagbemi, 1988, p.136). It was considered that competence in administration and management contributes little to promotional prospects.

Satisfaction with other aspects of the job

Apart from primary duties, five other aspects of university teachers' jobs were considered in ascertaining the level of job satisfaction or dissatisfaction. As indicated earlier, the areas where the university teachers were least satisfied with their jobs were pay and promotional prospects. The statistics in Tables 3 and 4 show gross discontent with these aspects of jobs. The question must be asked, 'Why are such a large percentage of teachers dissatisfied with both their pay and promotional prospects?'

Some insight was gained from factors that respondents listed as contributing most to their dissatisfaction. On promotion, for example, factors most frequently listed included, the criteria for promotion, the bias in favour of quantity instead of quality of publications, the relative neglect of teaching and administrative responsibilities when considering promotion, the scarcity of vacancies at professorial level, and a lack of clearly stated promotion policies. On salary, complaint seems to centre on procedures for determining salary increases and the inadequacy of the salary levels to enable a desired standard of living.

The subjects of pay and promotion are related in that, an institution without the necessary financial resources, may not be able to approve vacancies to which academics may be promoted. Limited financial resources may therefore be at the root of some of the complaints on pay and promotion, as is government policy on public-sector pay. However, institutional management could have a role to play in minimising staff dissatisfaction—complaints about a lack of clear promotion policies or unclear promotion criteria are areas where the management of some universities could improve their performance.

Pay and promotion should be a priority for management consideration, because the consequences of low levels of job satisfaction are undesirable in institutions. Nicholson and Miljus, found, for example, that universities with a large number of staff with low levels of job satisfaction could experience a high turnover rate (1972, p.840). Although some turnover is perhaps needed to prevent stagnation, a high turnover rate is costly to the reputation of a university and to the well-being of students. Similarly, organisational commitment and productivity may suffer due to low levels of job satisfaction. A mediating factor to a high turnover rate is, however, the overall levels of unemployment. Three other aspects of the university teachers' jobs examined were the head of unit's supervision, co-workers' behaviour, and the physical conditions/working facilities at universities.

On colleagues' behaviour, some 70 per cent of respondents were satisfied, very satisfied, or extremely satisfied. This indicates few widespread inter-personal problems among academics. This finding of a collegial and friendly atmosphere is useful, because academics perform several functions jointly, especially in committee groups. However, the satisfaction derived from the head of unit's supervision, although satisfactory, was not as high as the satisfaction obtained from interaction with colleagues. Moreover, about one out of every three respondents expressed some dissatisfaction with the supervision or behaviour of their head who, in the survey, could be a head of department, a dean of a faculty, a director of a school, or a provost of a college.

Again, this seems to be an area where performance could be improved. Although some universities have indeed introduced professional managers in purely administrative jobs superior to academic managers (Eggins, 1994, p.3), some activities, such as post-graduate admissions, or academic recruitment, are still better handled by academics who know what qualities they are seeking. In matters concerning the behaviour of administrative heads, some form of professional or specialised management training for office-holders can be recommended. This recognises the fact that some professors find themselves in managerial jobs by virtue of the fact that they were excellent researchers, but some may not necessarily be good managers. For greater effectiveness, managerial training is useful to such a category of academic managers.

University teachers were generally satisfied with the physical conditions and the working facilities found in their institutions. More than half of academic staff members were satisfied with these aspects. Here again, with almost one out of every three academics expressing dissatisfaction on this matter, this is surely an area where universities need to improve. With increases in numbers of students and staff, existing facilities will need to be expanded and improved if the level of the workers' job satisfaction is to be sustained. This calls for an increased funding of higher education by government.

Although increased funding is a common denominator towards solving deterioration or congestion identified in the use of facilities, the role that management can play in planning and executing strategies designed to optimise the use of available resources cannot be underestimated.

Measure of job satisfaction

Stated briefly, measuring the level of job satisfaction is an important task for a researcher. Basically there are two major types of job satisfaction measures: single and multiple-item measures. However these measures are not exclusive and both of them are sometimes used in a single study. Single-item measures typically ask a question such as, 'On the whole would you say you are satisfied or dissatisfied with the work you do?' and its variant, 'All in all, would you say you are satisfied or dissatisfied with your job?' (Quinn, et al., 1974, p.51).

A respondent may then be presented with a scale of measure from satisfaction to dissatisfaction or vice versa. Multiple-item measures, ask respondents to rate various aspects of their job on a scale running from certain levels of dissatisfaction to certain levels of satisfaction. The revised job descriptive index (Smith et al., 1985) and Oshagbemi's study of the job satisfaction of university teachers (1996; 1997a; 1997b; 1997c; 1998; 2003a; 2003c; 2013) provide examples of general-item measures of job satisfaction.

Although literature on the topic of job satisfaction is extensive, results obtained from empirical studies are often a function of the measure of job satisfaction employed. Although there are popular single-item and general multiple-item measures of job satisfaction, there are often specific tailor-made multiple measures of ascertaining the job satisfaction of specified workers. The choice of what measure to use in ascertaining the job satisfaction of a given occupational group is therefore sometimes problematic in terms of information desired and the ease of comparing results with those from different occupations.

This study sets out to compare the results of two research instruments employed to investigate the job satisfaction of university teachers. The aim is to compare the relative effectiveness of the two research instruments in the investigation of the job satisfaction of the workers. Ultimately, one is interested in evaluating the overall superiority, if any, of one measure of job satisfaction over the other. Towards this end, a widely used general measure to ascertain the job satisfaction of workers is employed and the results from this aspect of the study were compared with results from a tailor made measure of ascertaining the job satisfaction of university teachers. Results from the two sets of studies are presented and discussed.

It should be pointed out that studies into measures of job satisfaction are relatively few. A search of relevant articles through the Institute of Scientific Information Social Sciences database revealed that only seven articles were published between 1981 and 1997, both years inclusive. The search used 'measures of job satisfaction' as words in a title. When the search used 'measures of job satisfaction' as words in a title, keywords or an abstract, a total of 23 hits were recorded. This shows that relatively little has been written on the measurement of job satisfaction although there are extensive publications on the subject of job satisfaction itself.

The work by Thompson et al. (1997) focused on a synthesis of research findings on job satisfaction carried out within educational organisations. However, their review did not focus on measures of job satisfaction. Rather, it synthesised empirical findings on job satisfaction published in the first 26 volumes of *Educational Administration Quarterly*. Malinowska-Tabaka (1987) set out to establish a general job satisfaction/dissatisfaction scale for four professional groups (teachers, doctors, lawyers and engineers) and to discuss the importance of the different components of their job satisfaction/dissatisfaction scales. The general level of job satisfaction among three of the professions was found to be similar, except that for teachers, for whom it was slightly lower. There was no presentation of a conceptual scale of general applicability for the measurement of job satisfaction.

In his study, Pollard (1996) found that a single-item indicator offered a less comprehensive explanation of job satisfaction than did the four and seven-item indicators. The results of his study underlined that more attention needs to be paid to measurement issues if a reliable and valid understanding of job satisfaction among various professional workers is to be expected. Scarpello and Campbell (1983), by contrast, concluded that a single-item measure of overall job satisfaction was preferable to a scale that is based on the sum of specific job facet satisfactions. Since the publication of their article, however, the acceptance of single-item measures has not increased for a variety of reasons. Among these reasons, is the view, often expressed, that one cannot estimate the internal consistency of single-item measures, and this alone is sufficient reason to limit or avoid their use. Additionally, for psychological constructs, the use of single-item measures is typically discouraged, because they are presumed to have a low reliability.

Wanous et al. (1997) presented a study in which single-item measures of overall job satisfaction are correlated with scales measuring overall job satisfaction. Their finding seems to bolster their argument that a single-item measure of overall job satisfaction is acceptable. The authors suggested that the measurement of change in overall job satisfaction is one example of a research question suggesting the use of single-item measure. Nevertheless, the authors argue that there are still good reasons for preferring scales to single items and that the appropriateness of either a single or multiple-item measure of job satisfaction for a particular piece of research should always be evaluated.

The research reported here was designed to enable a comparison between a single and a multiple-item measure of job satisfaction. To measure the level of satisfaction of university teachers, respondents were asked to answer four questions concerning job satisfaction. The questions are given in Table 5. They have frequently been used in the past as measures of satisfaction; see, for example, Larkin (1990) and Oshagbemi (1995). An aggregate score of 20 on the four questions indicates that one is very satisfied with one's job. An aggregate score of four suggests that an individual is very dissatisfied. Table 5 gives the interpretation of the scores in terms of an individual's level of job satisfaction. The results from this instrument are designated as a 'single measure' in comparison to the second instrument described below.

Table 5: Job satisfaction test

I. Which one of the following indicates how much of the time you feel satisfied with your job:

1. Never
2. Seldom
3. About half of the time
4. Most of the time
5. All of the time

II. Which one of the following statements best describes how you feel about your job?

1. I hate it.
2. I dislike it.
3. I am indifferent to it.
4. I like it.
5. I love it.

III. Which one of the following statements best describes how you feel about changing your current job?

1. I would quit this job at once if I could.
2. I would like to change my job soon.
3. I am not sure if I would exchange my present job for a similar one.
4. I am not eager to change my job, but I would do so if I could get a better job.
5. I would not exchange my job for any other.

IV. Which one of the following statements best describes how you think you compare with other people?

1. No one dislikes his/ her job more than I dislike mine.
2. I dislike my job more than most people dislike theirs.
3. I like my job about as well as most people like theirs.
4. I like my job better than most people like theirs.
5. No one likes his/ her job better than I like mine.

Your job satisfaction measure: add up your score for the four questions. Match your total score with the appropriate category to find your job satisfaction measure.

Score	Job satisfaction level
20–17	Very satisfied
16–13	Satisfied
12	Indifferent
11–8	Dissatisfied
7–4	Very dissatisfied

To measure the job satisfaction of university teachers on particular aspects of their jobs, sections of a questionnaire comprising eight basic job elements and some demographic questions were introduced. The job elements are: teaching, research, administration and management, present pay, promotion, supervision/supervisor behaviour, co-workers' behaviour, and physical conditions/working facilities. Respondents were asked to indicate the level of satisfaction or dissatisfaction derived from each of the eight aspects of their jobs. The scale ranged from 1 to 7 representing 1 = 'extremely dissatisfied', 4 = 'indifferent', 7 = 'extremely satisfied', with all criteria being equally weighted (see section B of the appendix).

It is this questionnaire that is considered a multiple-item measure of job satisfaction. The results of the research instruments (single- vs multiple-item measures) form a central discussion in this chapter. The question is; which of the two research instruments provides superior results? To provide an answer to this question, the results of the research instruments are evaluated and judgement passed on their comparative value (Oshagbemi, 1999b).

General measure of job satisfaction

Table 6 is a summary of an analysis of the responses to the job satisfaction test that was used to estimate the level of general job satisfaction of university teachers.

Table 6: An analysis of responses to the job satisfaction test

(1) *The time you feel satisfied with your job.*

	Percent
Never	0.9
Seldom	10.0
About half of the time	37.3
Most of the time	49.5
All of the time	2.4
	100.0

(3) *Your feelings about changing your current job.*

	Percent
Would quit at once if I could	8.6
Would like to change job soon	9.5
Not sure/undecided	13.2
Not eager to change job	49.5
Would not exchange job for anything	19.2
	100.0

(2) *Statements describing how you feel about your job.*

	Percent
I hate it	0.9
I dislike it	7.8
I am indifferent to it	8.9
I like it	66.3
I love it	16.0
	100.0

(4) *How you think your feelings compare with others.*

	Percent
No one dislikes his/her job more than I dislike mine	0.0
I dislike my job more than most people dislike theirs	5.0
I like my job as well as most people like theirs	34.5
I like my job better than most people like theirs	59.6
No one likes his/her job better than I like mine	0.9
	100.0

A summary of responses to the job satisfaction test

Score	Percentage	Job satisfaction level
20–17	19	Very satisfied
16–13	64	Satisfied
12 3	11	Indifferent
11–8	3	Dissatisfied
7–4	100	Very dissatisfied
All responses		

From Table 6, it is seen that slightly more than 50 per cent of the respondents were satisfied with their jobs most of the time or all of the time, and approximately 90 per cent of the respondents were satisfied with their jobs about half, or more, of the time. About eight out of every ten respondents liked or loved their jobs, and approximately 70 per cent of the university teachers were either, not eager to change their job, or would not exchange their job for any other. Some 35 per cent of university teachers felt that they liked their job at about the same level as others liked their job, and approximately 60 per cent of the academics believe they prefer their job. In essence, some 95 per cent of university teachers indicate that they like their job as much or better than other jobs.

For general comparative purposes, and perhaps for a better overall picture of the university teachers' general satisfaction levels, the statistics at the bottom of Table 6 were prepared from the general analysis presented at the top of the page. The information at the bottom represents a summary of responses to the job satisfaction test. It shows the percentage of the respondents who were satisfied, dissatisfied or indifferent. It is clear from the table that 19 per cent were very satisfied, and 64 per cent were satisfied, giving a total of 83 per cent of the respondents who were, at least, satisfied with their job. Similarly, 3 per cent of the respondents were very dissatisfied and 11 per cent were dissatisfied giving a total of 14 per cent who were, at least, dissatisfied. About 3 per cent of the respondents were indifferent in terms of satisfaction or dissatisfaction with their job.

Compared with accountants, (Larkin, 1990, pp.20-24), university teachers seemed to possess a higher level of job satisfaction—72 per cent versus 83 per cent. Compared with a series of surveys on job satisfaction conducted in the USA between 1954 and 1973 (Quinn et al., 1974), where the level of workers' job satisfaction ranged between 81 and 92 per cent, the picture conveyed by the results of the job satisfaction survey of university teachers is satisfactory. It should be noted, however, that the general measures of job satisfaction used in Quinn's studies were similar in part to those in this.

Specific measure of job satisfaction

As indicated before, Tables 3 and 4 present a summary of responses to the job satisfaction questionnaire on particular aspects of the university teachers' job. The questionnaire was developed and administered together with the job satisfaction test. Findings from the job satisfaction questionnaire were compared with the findings from the job satisfaction test to generate the figures presented in Table 7.

Table 7: Comparison of the results of the single-versus multiple-item measure of job satisfaction

	Percentage satisfied	Percentage dissatisfied	Percentage indifferent
Single-item measure	83	14	3
Multiple-item measure	52	33	15
Difference ★	+31	-19	-12
Result	Overestimation	Underestimation	Underestimation

Notes: ★ Assumes that the multiple-item measure is closer to reality than the single-item measure, i.e. we take the multiple-item measure as the 'standard'.

The survey results are difficult to summarise in terms of the overall feelings of the respondents. Whereas the respondents seemed to be very satisfied with their main tasks, (i.e. teaching and research), they were clearly dissatisfied with some aspects of their job. The moderately high level of job satisfaction shown by university teachers may, in general, represent the feelings of most workers. However, to get the true average situation of the satisfaction of workers in all tasks, we take the mean of the average figures of each aspect of their job. It is the mean figures obtained from Table 6 that form the input to the multiple-item measure on Table 7.

Evaluation of the alternative methods

Table 7 is presented to discuss and appraise the alternative methods of single versus multiple-item measures. This table was prepared with the assumption that the multiple-item measure of job satisfaction is closer to reality than the single-item measure, the multiple-item measure is taken as the 'standard' from which deviations were recorded. Given this assumption, it can be seen from Table 7 that the single-item measure overestimates the percentage of people satisfied with their jobs by a wide margin of 31 per cent of the sample. Consequently, both the percentages of 'dissatisfied' and 'indifferent' academics were grossly underestimated. There are thus clear differences in the results obtained from the two measures used for the same study.

From Table 7, it can be seen that only 52 per cent of academics in UK universities are satisfied with their job, and as many as 33 per cent are dissatisfied. The remaining 15 per cent of staff show indifference. This means that the proportion of dissatisfied and indifferent academics is approximately the same as the proportion of academics who were satisfied with their jobs (48% v 52%). The interpretation is that, although academics are very satisfied with some tasks, overall, their satisfaction is only moderately high. It can be improved. Figures from the table show that single-item measures tend to exaggerate the results obtained for satisfaction whereas they underestimate results obtained for those workers who are dissatisfied and for those who show indifference. This shows single-item measures to be less reliable estimators of job satisfaction when compared to multiple measures of the same phenomenon.

A single-item measure of job satisfaction, such as the one used in this study, has advantages. Perhaps the greatest of these is the simplicity of the measure and its applicability to miscellaneous occupations. Thus, whether one is investigating the job satisfaction of pilots, solicitors or managers, the single-item measure of job satisfaction may be administered. This feature of simplicity, in turn, outlines its use in comparative studies, especially when the intention is to compare the job satisfaction of workers of one occupation with those of another. It also renders a measure of value when comparing the job satisfaction of workers in one country with those from a different country. Applicability of the single-item measure, over different time spans, is also an advantage that recommends its use.

There are also drawbacks to using a single-item measure of job satisfaction, and these can be summarised as the brevity of information obtained. Statistics obtained measure overall satisfaction in general terms without an opportunity to record satisfaction or dissatisfaction level on specific aspects of the same job. In essence, only the 'average' job satisfaction level is revealed, without the opportunity of knowing the composition of the average statistics.

Single-item derived job satisfaction levels are often of little value to managers who are interested in taking some action towards improving the level of job satisfaction of workers in their organisations. This is because single-item measures of job satisfaction do not reveal areas of strength or weakness of an organisation in terms of aspects of its operations which workers enjoy or do not enjoy. In essence, therefore, the single-item statistics of job satisfaction fail to give a 'report card' describing the success and/or failures of managers in ensuring that the job satisfaction of their workers remains reasonably high. Wanous et al. (1997) suggested that the appropriateness of single-item measures for a particular piece of research should always be evaluated. The authors further suggest that if neither the research question nor the research situation suggests the use of a single-item job satisfaction measure then choosing a well-constructed scale is sensible.

There are common problems with single-question measures of overall job satisfaction.

Firstly, there are problems of measurement: this has to do with the fact that different job satisfaction measures have different points at which discontent begins to register—the 'threshold of discontent'. The threshold of discontent depends on a number of factors, but there is one important conclusion. The most frequently used subjective measures of job satisfaction, for example, a question such as 'All in all, would you say you are satisfied or dissatisfied with your job?' tend to produce the highest estimate of satisfied workers (Quinn et al., 1974, pp.51-52).

Secondly, there tends to be a defensive reaction by workers to questions about job satisfaction. For example, workers may feel that being dissatisfied is their own fault as a result of having chosen the wrong job, or not bothering to do anything to get another one, or for a variety of other reasons. They may, for example, view their attitude to job satisfaction as reflecting poorly on their own decision-making abilities.

Thirdly, workers' reactions to job satisfaction questions may indicate an attempt to rationalise the problems they may face at work, especially if they are not able or willing to change their job. They may, for example, demand less of their job if they find a prolonged state of chronic dissatisfaction uncomfortable. The consequence is that such workers may report that they are satisfied with their present work when in fact they may not be!

In addition to these problems of measuring job satisfaction, there are problems of interpretation. Absolute levels of job satisfaction are much more difficult to determine than relative ones. Although researchers continue to search for an acceptable international measure of job satisfaction (Misener et al., 1996), the three problems of measurement discussed above suggest that no sure way has yet been devised for determining absolute levels of job satisfaction. However, although existing measures of job satisfaction provide questionable estimates of absolute levels of satisfaction, they are useful for comparing the satisfaction of workers in different occupations, at different times, in different demographic groups, and at different levels of hierarchy.

In evaluating multiple-item measures of job satisfaction, one must bear in mind that these are often tailor-made questionnaires appropriate to particular jobs. Thus, in evaluating the job satisfaction of university teachers, we designed a measure to record their satisfaction levels on important aspects of their job, their pay, promotions, supervision, co-workers' behaviour and physical conditions or working facilities arising from their job. One advantage of such measures is that they are relevant and they often reveal differences in job satisfaction levels derived from performing different parts of the same job. A picture of the overall satisfaction level from all tasks can also be ascertained by computing an average of the individual averages of identified tasks. Thus, the average statistics of one worker can be compared with another to find out which worker is, on the whole, more satisfied with his or her job.

When multiple-item job satisfaction measures are used, the information generated can provide managers with data on action to be initiated to, improve the overall job satisfaction of workers. It also informs managers on aspects of operations that workers enjoy and that should, as far as possible, be sustained. In essence, multiple-item job satisfaction measures help managers to improve their human and organisational management.

There are no disadvantages to multiple-item measures of job satisfaction as such except that specifics may sometimes make a general perception of workers' job satisfaction level difficult to ascertain. As a research tool, however, multiple-item measures of job satisfaction are more difficult to conceptualise and formulate and therefore tend to be more costly to produce when compared with single-item measures. Because single-item measures are relatively simple and short, they should perhaps accompany most multiple-item measures of job satisfaction studies. In this way, meaningful comparisons of job satisfaction studies can be greatly enhanced. Even then, factors responsible for job satisfaction or dissatisfaction may differ from one study to another, although the same or different satisfaction levels may be reported. In essence, therefore, a thorough understanding and description of the job satisfaction of an occupational group would also deal with the need to explain or interpret resulting job satisfaction statistics.

Although researchers continue to investigate the possibility of a uniform international measure of job satisfaction (Misener et al., 1996; Mueller and McCloskey, 1990), the differences in organisational culture and levels of economic and social development that exist in various countries make the adoption of a universal measure of job satisfaction unlikely.

Summary and conclusions

A general picture of job satisfaction and dissatisfaction of university teachers in the UK has been given. The survey found that, on the whole, university teachers were generally fairly satisfied with their jobs. They were particularly satisfied with teaching and, to a lesser extent, research; they also derived satisfaction from interaction with colleagues. This suggests harmonious relationships in dealings with co-workers and in the joint performance of duties.

Because promotional and salary policies seem to be at the very core of the job satisfaction problems of university teachers, it is suggested that these are areas where the internal management of universities may be able to improve their performance. University administrators need to rationalise salary and promotional policies in a justifiable manner and should involve the academics in both the conceptualisation and the implementation of procedures. University teachers should be made fully aware of expectations, how they are evaluated, the criteria for evaluation and salary increases, and who determines promotions and salary levels. There should be little room for administrative ambiguity, or secrecy that can, often inevitably, lead to unhealthy suspicion.

Increased government funding can, of course, significantly improve both the pay and promotional prospects of university teachers. Such action will enhance the job satisfaction of university teachers, and will facilitate a system that operates at a greater productive capacity.

Given changes in the higher education sector (e.g. financial stringency or the introduction of systems to monitor performance), these findings on the job satisfaction of university teachers may be regarded as a little surprising. In personal interaction with some academics, most of them seem to believe that the spate of government changes in higher education policies have resulted in, among other things, low levels of job satisfaction in university teachers. There have also been suggestions in the media that academic staff are less than satisfied with their jobs. For example, the following statement appeared in the media:

> Academics all over the world feel underpaid, unappreciated, and alienated from the administrators who run their institutions. Those in the United Kingdom feel this more strongly than most of their foreign counterparts, according to a survey of 20,000 university lecturers and professors from 14 countries (*Times Higher Education Supplement,* 1994, p.1).

This investigation shows that the belief that UK academics may not be generally satisfied with their jobs seems to have been more widely publicised than well documented. This survey shows no evidence that university teachers are generally dissatisfied with their jobs. Although there are areas of dissatisfaction, on the whole, the picture is not at all gloomy. Despite speculation to the contrary, UK academics seem to be, on the whole, well satisfied with their jobs.

Unfortunately no comparative studies are available to establish whether, compared with, say, 10 years ago, UK academics' level of job satisfaction is lower, higher, or much the same. It is possible that, notwithstanding the apparently fairly high level of current job satisfaction of university teachers, academics enjoyed a higher job satisfaction in the past. In this event, the job-satisfaction level enjoyed by academics may have, in reality, declined even though still considered as satisfactory.

It is possible that satisfaction with certain aspects of the job may have declined over time, whereas satisfaction with other aspects may have actually increased, yielding little net change in overall satisfaction. There is certainly no evidence to suggest that the aggregate level of the job satisfaction of academics is rising. Although there may well be improvements in the quality of employment, workers' rising expectations could, for example, counteract the effects of such improvements.

Part Two of the study reported in this chapter aims to compare the effectiveness of two research instruments used to measure the job satisfaction of university teachers. In the single-item study, respondents were asked simple questions about satisfaction with their job, such as: how often they feel satisfied with their jobs, their feelings about changing their current job, statements such as 'hate' or 'love' describing how they feel about their job and how they think their feelings compare with others (see Table 5). In the multiple-item measure, the respondents were asked questions not only on their satisfaction with teaching, research and administration and management, but also on satisfaction with their pay, promotions, co-workers' behaviour, supervisor behaviour and physical conditions or working facilities which exist in their organisations. The respondents' answers were analysed and compared for comprehensive information and consistency of opinions.

Results of the study show that the multiple-item measure of job satisfaction was more detailed in terms of aspects of the respondents' jobs where information was available. In addition, the measure was useful in comparing tasks or aspects of the same job. However, if a comparison of the job satisfaction of workers in different occupations were desired, a single-item job satisfaction measure may be preferable because it tends to eliminate the specifics and peculiarities of specific jobs. It is, therefore, suggested that, where possible, both single as well as multiple-item measures of job satisfaction should be used in the same study.

In discussing the results, the complementary nature of the two measures of job satisfaction is apparent. It is, therefore, felt that both measures are superior to either of them used alone. If a choice of only one method must be made, the choice of which method to use would depend largely on the objectives of a research project. In comparative studies, the single-item measure has obvious advantages, whereas in organisational or occupational studies, tailor made multiple-item measures tend to provide more comprehensive information.

CHAPTER 4

Content Analysis of Job Satisfaction and Dissatisfaction

Introduction

IT IS DESIRABLE, IN this chapter, to focus the discussion on factors that university teachers say contribute to their satisfaction and/or dissatisfaction and discuss these in the light of two-factor theory and the situational occurrences theory of job satisfaction. The two theories are first explained and their application in this study then considered (Oshagbemi, 1997c). The chapter probes explanations for job satisfaction or dissatisfaction in higher education using content analytical methodologies. It finds that teaching and research-related activities contribute significantly to both job satisfaction and dissatisfaction among university teachers. It is also found that several miscellaneous dimensions of the job of teachers, such as relative job security and changes in university funding mechanisms, contribute to satisfaction and dissatisfaction respectively.

Two-factor theory and situational occurrences theory

Herzberg et al. (1959) expounded the dual-factor theory of job satisfaction that states there are two groups of factors that determine job satisfaction or job dissatisfaction. Herzberg's (1966, 1968) two-factor theory suggests that only job content-related facets (e.g., achievement, responsibility, the work itself) lead to satisfaction. By constrast, job context-related factors (e.g., pay, security, working conditions) lead to job dissatisfaction but not to satisfaction. As pointed out by King (1970), the two-factor theory is not entirely clear, and there are, at least, five possible interpretations of the theory (1970, pp.18-19). Indeed, several reviews of Herzberg-related literature have cast serious doubt on the validity of this theory (House and Wigdor, 1967).

Recently, Quarstein et al. (1992) posited the situational occurrences theory of job satisfaction which contends that job satisfaction is determined by two factors, as does Herzberg's theory. However, as the authors indicate, this is the only similarity between the two theories. The situational occurrences theory argues that job satisfaction is a function of situational occurrences and situational characteristics and that any given factor, for example pay or recognition, can result in either job satisfaction or dissatisfaction. It does not distinguish between job content or job context-related factors. Rather, it posits that overall job satisfaction could be predicted from a combination of situational occurrences (which can be positive e.g. coffee/tea breaks or negative e.g. insufficient paper towels in rest rooms), and situational characteristics (which are stable, such as pay, and working conditions) rather than by either situation alone.

There are problems with a consistent interpretation of Herzberg's theory (King, 1970; Burke, 1966; Lindsay, 1967; Tang and Gilbert, 1995). Quarstein and colleagues' theory (1992) neglects the role of personal factors, such as age and education in influencing job satisfaction and the theory is yet to be independently tested. Identification and discussion of the factors, considerations or aspects of university teachers' jobs that contribute most to their satisfaction and/or dissatisfaction follows in this review. In this manner, a valid summary can be given of elements which workers themselves claim contribute to their job satisfaction and job dissatisfaction.

Factors that contribute to satisfaction

Table 8 summarises the content analysis based on respondents' list of factors, considerations or aspects of jobs which contribute to their satisfaction. It shows clearly that teaching and research-related factors contribute most to teachers' satisfaction because these two factors account for about 50 per cent of their overall satisfaction. Indeed, it would seem from the analysis that it is the primary aspects of university teachers' jobs that mostly explain their job satisfaction and not other considerations such as administration and managerial duties, present pay, promotion, head of unit's supervision/behaviour, or their physical conditions/working facilities.

The list of teaching-related items showing the job satisfaction of respondents include, but are not limited to the following: student enthusiasm, admissions, pleasant students, meeting young people, contacts with students, high degree of autonomy in teaching and course development, helping students to pass examinations and do well, opportunity to work with and learn from students some of whom have responsible jobs in developing countries, student feedback on courses, supervision of student projects, student advance in understanding, type of courses taught, autonomy in content of teaching, helping mature students to achieve more than they thought they could, the ability to enthuse students through teaching, contribution to student development, respect from students and developing courses.

Table 8: Content analysis based on respondents' list of factors, considerations or aspects of their jobs which contribute to their satisfaction

Category	Percentage of occurrence
Teaching	25.0
Research	25.0
Administration and management	1.0
Present pay	1.0
Promotion	0.5

Head of department's supervision/behaviour	2.0
Co-workers' behaviour	12.0
Physical conditions/working facilities	6.0
Other aspect of job	27.5
Total	*100.0*

The list of research-related items indicated as contributory to the satisfaction of teachers include: research success in terms of publications, academic freedom, opportunities to write and publish, collaboration with colleagues, opportunities to attend conferences, research recognition, research challenges, success in research rating, finding out new things in own research area, attending interesting seminars, research funds which give a certain amount of financial autonomy, supervising PhD students, setting up research seminars, research collaboration with other departments, rewarding intellectual content of work, available research time, opportunity to become well-known through published research work, sabbatical leave, supervising interesting postgraduate projects, winning grant funding, and joint research work with a foreign university.

The list of teaching and research-related factors were written by the academics themselves and thus represents reality and not the researcher's own classification or itemisation of possible explanations for the teachers' satisfaction with core tasks.

There was, however, a list of other aspects of the university teachers' jobs that explained about 28 per cent of their satisfaction and thus marginally accounts for a higher satisfaction level than either teaching or research considered individually. These are: relative job security, opportunity for consultancy, freedom of your life style, time flexibility in terms of working hours, secretarial and technical assistance, foreign travel, opportunity to work at home, contact with industry through consultancy, opportunity for some self-development, being recognised for contributions, possibility of early retirement, long holidays, no direct boss, working with young people, retirement benefits, very varied nature of work, access to computer networks and library facilities.

This finding shows that considerations other than a worker's core activities can often be very important in determining total job satisfaction. Thus, consistent with the findings of Quarstein et al.'s (1992), situational occurrences may be important in assessing overall job satisfaction and not just situational characteristics alone.

The content analysis also revealed that administration and managerial duties, present pay, promotions, and head of department supervision/behaviour together contribute to less than 5 per cent of the total list of factors which university teachers themselves say contribute to their satisfaction. It shows that the teachers do not consider these aspects of their jobs to be relatively important in affecting their satisfaction. Why? One explanation could be the teachers' relative inability to change or significantly influence these factors, which they may then accept as given. By contrast they still enjoy relative independence in deciding their teaching and research activities.

It is interesting to observe that considerations such as co-workers' behaviour and physical conditions/working facilities explain close to 20 per cent of the workers' satisfaction as listed in their questionnaires. It shows the relative importance of these variables in affecting job satisfaction. The list of items to explain their job satisfaction with these two aspects include: the stimulating environment, a beautiful campus, good library facilities, clerical assistance, good physical conditions, technical support, facilities for teaching, computing facilities, good social environment, pleasant working colleagues, value team work, competent co-workers, congeniality of colleagues, relationship with support/technical staff, support by colleagues, (i.e. other academic staff), friendship of colleagues, collaboration with colleagues, commitment of colleagues and happy collegial relationships.

Factors that contribute to dissatisfaction

Table 9 summarises the results of content analysis based on respondents' list of factors, considerations or aspects of their jobs that contribute to dissatisfaction. The main aspects of the teachers work, teaching and research together explain about 30 per cent of their dissatisfaction. An examination of respondents' questionnaires reveals a list of teaching-related items that explains their job dissatisfaction: sharp increases in class size, badly thought-out procedures for course evaluation that seem inapplicable to the teaching/learning environment, public stance of university that claims to value teaching and administrative activity—(this is as it should be but does not reflect reality), little recognition of teaching skills, demands of individual students, student expansion without commensurate increase in resources, marking answer scripts, amount of marking and over assessment, falling quality of intake, increasing staff/student ratios, government interference with teaching, too many students, student attitude to learning (interest shown by students), emphasis on research at the expense of teaching and sheer amount of mechanical teaching and marking.

Similarly, the list of research-related items stated as contributory to the job dissatisfaction of university teachers include the following: inadequate time available for research, pressure to publish, erosion of time for research and personal development in specialist area, increasing difficulty/time spent in obtaining research grants, funding for research, difficulty in attracting able PhD students, necessity of applying for grant support, lack of research funds, insufficient time for research, the undue importance now attached to 'research', little time spent writing, research assessment exercises and lack of research facilities.

Table 9: Content analysis based on respondents' list of factors, considerations or aspects of their jobs which contribute to their dissatisfaction

Category	Percentage of occurrence
Teaching	16.0
Research	16.0
Administration and management	8.5
Present pay	6.5
Promotion	6.5
Head of department's supervision/	3.5
behaviour	2.5
Co-workers' behaviour	10.0
Physical conditions/working facilities	30.5
Other aspect of job	
Total	100.0

Contrary to Herzberg's theory, there are elements of the job itself being responsible for both job satisfaction and dissatisfaction. In the current study, aspects of both teaching and research were responsible for both job satisfaction and dissatisfaction.

There was, however, a list of other aspects of the university teachers' jobs that together explain about 30 per cent of their dissatisfaction and hence account for most of the total amount of dissatisfaction experienced from both teaching and research tasks. A sample from this list of items: lack of understanding from communication with university authorities, failure to provide agreed job description, authoritarian management structure, lack of consultation and communication from top down, government policy towards universities, working hours, lack of co-ordination in management, no promotion unless applied for, the lack of proper departmental strategy on teaching and research, retirement benefits, excessive bureaucracy, lack of leadership from the centre of the university, inconsistency in planning, location in centre of city, changes in university funding mechanisms, not being able to retire at 60 with full benefits, lack of time to think, split responsibilities between administration, teaching and research is difficult to manage, and indifferent, incompetent and inefficient management.

Possibly because administration and management were not rated as primary duties, these tasks were not regarded as constituting particularly high dissatisfaction factors. Interestingly, present pay, promotions, head of departments' supervision and co-workers' behaviour together explain less than 20 per cent of university teachers' job satisfaction. Why? Although these elements do not contribute highly to job satisfaction they do not explain significant job dissatisfaction either. Whereas co-workers' behaviour contributes about 12 per cent to satisfaction, it explains less than 3 per cent of workers' dissatisfaction. Again, contrary to Herzberg's theory, here the same factor contributes to both job satisfaction and dissatisfaction although at different levels. Considering the complexity of the decisions relating to both satisfaction and dissatisfaction, it would seem that the two-factor theory is really an over-simplification of reality in today's organisations.

Summary and conclusions

This study has employed a content analytical methodology to investigate contributory factors to the job satisfaction and dissatisfaction of teachers in higher education. The study found that, on an individual factor basis, the same factor contributes significantly to both satisfaction and dissatisfaction. For example, teaching and research each contributes about 25 per cent to satisfaction and about 16 per cent to dissatisfaction. This indicates that the job of the academics, i.e. teaching and research, contributes to and explains about 50 per cent of their satisfaction. Rather interestingly, it also found that the teachers' job explains over 30 per cent of their job dissatisfaction! In essence, the findings show that the university teachers' job of teaching and research contributes significantly to both their job satisfaction and dissatisfaction. Can the same factor contribute to satisfaction for some workers and contribute to dissatisfaction for some others? In the reality of the modern work environment, there is no reason why such a situation cannot occur. After all, people's interests and abilities differ.

As Gruneberg and Startup (1978) suggest, dissatisfaction with research, for example, might not mean dissatisfaction with the intrinsic aspects of the research process itself, but with failure to be involved in the research process. This means that although the research process itself may be satisfying to those who are involved, failure to get involved may be reported as dissatisfaction with research. The problem, in that case, may not be with the particular task, that is research *per se,* but with the individual's inability to allocate enough time to research.

In addition, lack of success with research, may also signal dissatisfaction with the task. After all, it is difficult to enjoy research when one is not successful at it. It seems that both the quality of the research product and satisfaction with the process, are of importance to an individual's satisfaction with his or her job as a whole.

Aspects of the university teachers' job which are difficult to classify comprise miscellaneous dimensions of their tasks that also contribute significant percentages of about 28 per cent and 31 per cent to their job satisfaction and dissatisfaction respectively (see Tables 8 and 9). This finding supports the view that the job of workers alone may not fully explain their job satisfaction or dissatisfaction. Contrary to the two-factor theory, there are situational occurrences about a job which are often important in determining overall job satisfaction or dissatisfaction.

These findings do not support Herzberg's (1966) theory that states that the factors that lead to job satisfaction are separate and distinct from those that lead to job dissatisfaction. Rather, the results of this investigation seem to support the situational occurrences theory which argues that any given factor, for example, the work itself or salary, can result in either job satisfaction or dissatisfaction. This means that overall job satisfaction can be improved if employers concentrate their efforts on both situational occurrences and situational characteristics rather than by either factor on its own. In effect, both 'hygienes' and motivators can contribute to job satisfaction or job dissatisfaction.

CHAPTER 5

Job Satisfaction Profiles of University Teachers

Introduction

THIS CHAPTER ENQUIRES WHETHER university teachers can be meaningfully grouped on the basis of the satisfaction levels they enjoy in the various aspects of their jobs. Using a cluster analytical procedure, UK university teachers were grouped into three divisions: 'happy workers', 'satisfied workers' and 'unhappy workers'. Although the happy workers (67%) and the satisfied workers (14%) form a majority of the workforce, suggestions are offered towards reducing the percentage of unhappy workers (19%) in higher education. In particular, this chapter focuses on this newer and possibly very useful approach to classifying workers, instead of the traditional method based on the criterion of rank alone. The chapter goes on to discuss the implications of this approach of grouping workers.

University teachers show wide variations in the satisfaction levels they enjoy for various dimensions of their jobs. For example, in this study, variations in job satisfaction levels were recorded by university teachers for the following criteria: research, teaching, administration and management, pay, promotion, co-workers' behaviour, head of department's behaviour, and facilities available in their institutions. The coefficient of variation obtained for some of the distributions of job satisfaction with some aspects of their jobs was higher than 100 per cent. It would be useful to enquire, therefore, whether in view of these variations, university teachers can be classified on the basis of the job satisfaction levels which they enjoy for various dimensions of their jobs.

A meaningful grouping should show whether there is an alternative, and possibly a very useful, way of classifying university teachers apart from the traditional approach based on the criterion of rank. It may also have implications for the management of some university activities such as pay and promotion, which are of concern to all groups of university teachers.

A further insight into discussions of worker effectiveness may also be gained and worker productivity better understood in relation to meaningful groupings using fairly comprehensive opinions of job satisfaction levels gauged from their likes or dislikes of aspects of their jobs.

This study confirms that university teachers can be usefully grouped on the basis of their job satisfaction levels on important aspects of their jobs. It describes the method for the classification, the criteria used, and the results.

The criteria used for classification

It is obvious that the nature of the groupings obtained will be a partial function of the criteria used and the methodology employed. Different criteria from ours and or a different methodology may produce different results. However, in order to produce a useful grouping, 'comprehensive' criteria incorporating the major elements of each job satisfaction measure should be made. A selection of such criteria that was used in our classification is listed below. The first part of the measures contains eight variables. What was being investigated was the extent of job satisfaction derived by each activity or consideration (see chapter 3).

1. research;
2. teaching;
3. administration and management;
4. pay;
5. promotion;
6. co-workers' behaviour;
7. head of department's behaviour; and
8. facilities available in their institutions.

To measure the level of general satisfaction of university teachers, a measure suitable for assessing the job satisfaction of other categories of workers was used. Here respondents were asked to answer four questions concerning job satisfaction.

Respondents were required to indicate:

1. An estimate of how much of the time they feel satisfied with their job.
2. Their love or hatred for their job.
3. Their feelings about changing their job.
4. How they compare with other workers on their likes or dislikes for their job.

These questions have been frequently used in the past as measures of satisfaction (see, for example, Larkin, 1990; Oshagbemi, 1995). The maximum and minimum total scores on the four questions were 20 and 4 respectively. This means that each question has a range of answers graded on scores from 5 to 1. An average score of 5 on the four questions indicates that one is very satisfied with one's job whereas a mean score of 1 suggests that an individual is very dissatisfied.

The 12 variables were given equal weight in the analyses.

Method and statistical analysis

It is obvious that the nature of the groupings obtained will be a partial function of the criteria used and the methodology employed. Different criteria from those adopted in the questionnaire or a different methodology from cluster analysis may produce different results. However, to produce a useful grouping, the satisfaction levels that university teachers derive from the various dimensions of their jobs were used.

Because the number of cases in this survey was large, a quick cluster analysis was used, which groups large numbers of cases efficiently and produces only one solution for the number of clusters requested (Anderberg, 1973; Wischart, 1982, 1987). Between three and eight different sets of cluster solutions were produced for examination to determine the optimum number of clusters consistent with the aim of avoiding very small and specialised clusters, (i.e. less than 10% of the total population, (Everitt, 1974; Lorr, 1983).

Only the three-cluster solution satisfies this condition from the six groups of clusters requested for examination and consideration. Each of the other cluster solutions produced at least two, and as many as five, clusters which were less than or equal to 10 per cent of the total population. The five-cluster solution followed the three-cluster solution with only one cluster less than 10 per cent and another cluster of 10 per cent of the total population.

The groups of university teachers

From the cluster analysis, three groups of university teachers were identified. Group 1 is named 'happy workers', Group 2 is named 'satisfied workers' and Group 3 is referred to as 'unhappy workers' based on characteristics of their job satisfaction levels on the eight identified aspects of their jobs. These groups of workers are described below (Oshagbemi, 1997a). Tables 10 and 11 present data that describes the group of university teachers and job satisfaction statistics of the groups of university teachers respectively.

Happy workers (Group 1)

This group, with 371 members, represents 67 per cent of the sample. They derive their name from the fact that they recorded the highest average satisfaction levels when all dimensions of their job were considered. This group was first for satisfaction levels enjoyed for five aspects of their job, namely: administration and management, pay, promotions, head of unit's supervision/behaviour and co-workers' behaviour. Happy workers came a narrow second on the satisfaction levels enjoyed on the remaining three aspects of their job: teaching, research, and working facilities/physical conditions which exist at their universities.

In addition, the happy workers came first on each of the following measures when compared with other groups of university workers in the sample: an estimate of how much of the time they feel satisfied with their job; their love or hatred for their job; their feelings about not changing their job; and how they compare with other workers on their likes or dislikes for their job.

Table 10 reveals that 63 per cent of the happy workers (Group 1) are male and 37 per cent are female. Distribution by rank shows that 54 per cent of the workers are lecturers, and 31 per cent are senior lecturers. Some 14 per cent of Group 1 workers are either professors or readers. The age distribution of happy workers reveals that slightly over 70 per cent of this group's members are in the 35-54 age bracket and about 14 per cent of members are older than 55.

About half of the respondents in this group had spent 10 years or less in their present universities and about 53 per cent had spent less than 15 years in higher education. Teachers in this group, as in other groups, are fairly normally distributed across all academic disciplines in the universities. About 60 per cent of members in the group are not currently in charge of any units and around 25 per cent of staff are administratively responsible for some units or groups. Again, the same pattern of distribution of leadership or management responsibility exists in the other two groups of university teachers described hereunder.

Table 10: Background information on the groups of university teachers

Characteristics	Group 1 (67%) Happy workers	Group 2 (14%) Satisfied workers	Group 3 (19%) Unhappy workers
Gender	%	%	%
Male	63	60	52
Female	37	40	48
Rank			
Lecturer	54	62	52
Senior lecturer	31	26	36
Reader	05	03	04
Professor	09	07	08
Other rank	01	02	00
Age			
00–34	14	13	15
35–44	36	31	36
45–54	36	35	42
55+	14	21	07
Leadership/management responsibility	61	64	69
Not currently in charge	25	27	23
In charge of some academic unit or group	11	08	06
Head of department	03	01	02
Other management posts, e.g. dean, director, provost, head of department			

Satisfied workers (Group 2)

This second group of university teachers is made up of 78 members and represents 14 per cent of the sample. This group is distinguished by high levels of satisfaction with the primary functions of teaching and research and with the organizational facilities which exist to enable them to carry out their tasks satisfactorily. The group's name derives from these features or characteristics. The group came first with regard to the satisfaction levels enjoyed for the following considerations: teaching, research, and facilities that exist in their universities.

Although satisfied workers are not as 'happy' as Group 1 members in overall considerations, they are most happy with their primary responsibilities. Satisfied workers came second to Group 1 workers in the satisfaction levels that they enjoy from co-workers' behaviour and from their present pay. These academics are further distinguished by the lowest satisfaction levels (among the three groups) derived from promotions within the university system and the supervisory behaviour of heads of departments and other units.

It is of interest that satisfied workers were second to happy workers in each of the following measures: an estimate of how much of the time they feel satisfied with their job, their love or hatred for their job, their feelings about not changing their job, and how they compare with other workers on their likes or dislikes for their job.

From data presented in Table 10, a description of satisfied workers (Group 2) can be made. Table 10 shows that, in this group, male members out-number female members by three to two. Lecturers and senior lecturers respectively represent 62 per cent and 26 per cent of members of this group. Readers and professors account for 10 per cent of the group membership.

About 40 per cent of group members had spent ten years or so either in their present university or in higher education. A distribution of the age of members shows that Group 2 has the oldest people with 21 per cent of its membership older than 55 years in comparison with 14 per cent of members of (Group 1) and 7 per cent of (Group 3). The academic disciplines of satisfied workers are, like those of happy workers, fairly normally distributed across all subject areas. Similarly, the percentage of persons within leadership or management responsibilities follows more or less identical patterns in all the three groupings.

Unhappy workers (Group 3)

The third group of workers has 105 members, and represents 19 per cent of the total sample.) There are a larger number of unhappy workers (Group 3), than satisfied workers (Group 2) but these groups combined are still smaller than half the size of happy workers (Group 1). Unhappy workers distinguish themselves by recording the lowest overall levels of job satisfaction; hence their name. They record the lowest satisfaction levels among the three groups of workers on all eight aspects of their jobs with the exception of the satisfaction levels for promotion and supervisors' behaviour in which they record higher satisfaction levels than those in Group 2, but not as high as the satisfaction levels recorded by happy workers (Group 1).

Relative to the other two groups, unhappy workers came last on the satisfaction levels they enjoy on each of the following measures: an estimate of how much of the time they feel satisfied with their job; their love or hatred for their job; their feelings about not changing their job; and how they compare with other workers on their likes or dislikes for their job. These results lend credibility to the cluster methodology.

A description of the group of unhappy workers can be made from data contained in Table 10. Information from Table 10 shows that whereas the proportion of females to males is 59 per cent in the first group (happy workers), 67 per cent in the second (satisfied workers), it is 92 per cent in the third group (unhappy workers). In essence, there were nearly as many female workers as there were males in this grouping—a sharp contrast to the proportion of females to males in the other two groupings and in the overall sample of university teachers. This result may suggest that female workers in universities tend to be less happy with their jobs when compared with their male counterparts. However, research results into gender differences in job satisfaction are not conclusive across all occupational groups. Whereas some research studies report gender differences, others do not (Mason, 1995; Olsen, et al., 1995).

Another distinguishing feature of unhappy workers (Group 3) is that it has the lowest per cent of workers aged over 55: happy workers (14 per cent), satisfied workers (21 per cent), unhappy workers 7 per cent. This finding indicates a possibility, indeed, a likelihood that, younger academics working in universities tend to be dissatisfied with their jobs when their satisfaction levels are compared with those of older workers. If so, this preliminary finding conforms to other results in the literature suggesting that there is some association between employee age and job satisfaction (see, for example, Mottaz, 1987; Luthans, and Thomas, 1989; Kong, Chye, and Hian, 1993).

The rank distribution of unhappy workers tends to follow the same pattern as those of the other two groups, as does leadership and management responsibility and the distribution of university teachers across academic disciplines. Additionally, the length of service of university teachers in this group, either in their present institution or in higher education, tends to be similar to the distribution patterns of the other two groups.

Table 11: Some job satisfaction statistics of the groups of university teachers

	Group 1 (67%) Happy workers			Group 2 (14%) Satisfied workers			Group 3 (19%) Unhappy workers		
	Mode	Median	Mean	Mode	Median	Mean	Mode	Median	Mean
Teaching	5	5	5.24	5	6	5.49	5	5	4.26
Research	5	5	4.69	6	5	4.90	5	5	4.35
Administration and management	5	4	4.23	3	3	3.00	4	4	3.54
Present pay	5	4	3.66	3	3	3.04	3	3	2.95
Promotions	4	4	3.85	1	2	2.23	3	3	2.77
Supervision/ supervisor behaviour	5	5	5.02	1	2	2.23	1	2	2.47
Co-workers' behaviour	5	5	5.09	5	5	4.99	3	3	3.63
Physical conditions/ working facilities	5	5	4.70	5	5	4.94	3	3	2.54
==========									
An estimate of how much of the time they feel satisfied with their job	4	4	3.57	4	3	3.30	3	3	3.01
Their love or hatred for their job	4	4	4.04	4	4	3.84	4	4	3.38
Their feelings about not changing their job	4	4	3.89	4	4	3.14	4	3	2.97
How they compare with other workers on their likes or dislikes for their job	4	4	3.66	4	4	3.44	3	3	3.33

Comparison of the groups of university teachers

This section compares the three groups of university teachers, using tests of significant differences (Table 12) and statistics from the cluster analysis on each aspect of their job (Table 11). This comparison brings out similarities and differences in the groups' job satisfaction levels in each dimension. A comparison is made between the three groups on the period of time they feel satisfied with their job, their love or hatred for their job, their feelings about not changing their job, and how they compare with other workers on their likes or dislikes for their job (Table 12).

Table 12: A comparative analysis of the groups of university teachers

	Happy and Satisfied Workers		Happy and Unhappy Workers		Satisfied and Unhappy Workers	
	T-Value	Result	T-Value	Result	T-Value	Result
Teaching	−1.73	NS	6.43	P<0.001	6.29	P<0.001
Research	−1.01	NS	1.86	NS	2.19	P<0.05
Administration and management	7.19	P<0.001	4.44	P<0.001	−2.54	P<0.05
Present pay	3.54	P≤0.001	4.29	P<0.001	0.40	NS
Promotions	10.89	P<0.001	6.80	P<0.001	−2.81	P<0.01
Supervision/ supervisor behaviour	19.35	P<0.001	15.97	P<0.001	−1.23	NS
Co-workers' behaviour	0.70	NS	10.81	P<0.001	7.68	P<0.001
Physical conditions/ working facilities	−1.69	NS	15.14	P<0.001	13.44	P<0.001
===						
An estimate of how much of the time they feel satisfied with their job	2.90	P<0.01	6.40	P<0.001	2.40	P<0.05
Their love or hatred for their job	1.91	NS	6.08	P<0.001	3.30	P≤0.001

| Their feelings about not changing their job | 4.69 | P<0.001 | 6.64 | P<0.001 | 0.87 | NS |
| How they compare with other workers on their likes or dislikes for their job | 2.72 | P<0.01 | 4.56 | P<0.001 | 1.14 | NS |

Comparison of groups on the primary functions

The primary functions of university teachers are teaching, research, and administration and management. The satisfaction derived from these tasks by the three identified groups is now considered in greater detail.

Teaching is an aspect of a university job that satisfies all three groups. Table 11 shows that the modal and median ratings by all groups were each 5 (signifying satisfaction with job) except the median rating of 6 (very satisfied) given to it by satisfied workers (Group 2). It should be noted that the mean rating for teaching by Group 2 was not statistically significant when compared with the rating of teaching by Group 1, because both groups rated teaching fairly highly. As seen in Table 12, however, the mean rating for teaching was statistically significant between the happy (Group 1) and unhappy (Group 3) workers and between the satisfied (Group 2) and unhappy workers. This result shows that teaching is rated relatively low by Group 3 workers compared within the ratings of the other two groups.

Research activity is another function accorded a modal and median rating of 5 (signifying satisfaction with the job) by the three groups of university teachers with the exception of a modal rating of 6 (signifying very satisfied with the job) given to research function by Group 2 workers. There were no significant differences between the group ratings for research except between Group 2 and Group 3 workers which is significant at the 95 per cent confidence level.

As with the teaching task, the job satisfaction rating of the research function is satisfactory for all groups of university teachers.

The function of administration and management is, however, rated differently from teaching and research tasks by the three groups of university teachers. Whereas Group 1 workers rated the function satisfactory, Group 3 workers scored it marginally unsatisfactory and Group 2 workers rated it as definitely unsatisfactory. In fact, the modal, median and mean rating by Group 2 coincided with dissatisfaction. The differences in ratings among the three groups are statistically significant (see Table 12).

Comparison of groups on other aspects of the job

In addition to satisfaction with the primary duties, there were five other aspects of university teacher's job that were used for the cluster analysis: satisfaction with pay, promotions, head of department's behaviour, co-workers' behaviour and facilities available in the universities. The three clustered groups are now compared with regard to each of these elements.

University pay was, overall, one of the least rated items contributing to teachers' job satisfaction. Group 1 workers rated pay with indifference whereas Group 2 members were not content with their pay. Group 3 workers were, indeed, very dissatisfied with a mean rating of less than 3 for satisfaction with pay. Although there was no statistical difference between Group 2 and Group 3 workers' ratings of pay, there were differences in rating between both of them and Group 1 workers. It should be noted that the modal and median rating of pay by both Group 2 and Group 3 workers was 3 (signifying dissatisfaction) whereas corresponding ratings by Group 1 members were 5(signifying satisfaction) and 4 (indicating indifference).

Promotion is an aspect of the job which, like pay, was not highly rated by university teachers who claim that promotion criteria and processes contribute to their job dissatisfaction. Happy workers (Group 1) rated promotion indifferently with modal and median value of 4, and a mean score of less than 4. However, this was the highest rating by any of the three groups. The modal and median rating of promotion by unhappy workers (Group 3) was 3 denoting dissatisfaction and the mean score was less than 3. The lowest rating of job satisfaction for promotion was a mean of slightly above 2 a modal value of 1 (signifying extreme dissatisfaction) and a median value of 2 (very dissatisfied). This very low rating was by Group 2 workers. The records on Table 12 show that the ratings made by the three groups were statistically significant when compared with one another. Thus the ratings made by each group for this task was not only low, but materially different from the ratings of other groups.

Head of unit's supervision or behaviour is an aspect of job where Group 1 workers were satisfied with a mean rating of slightly greater than 5. However, both Groups 2 and 3 were grossly dissatisfied with this aspect of the job, recording mean ratings of less than 2.5 each. This dissatisfaction is perhaps very well portrayed by the median and modal statistics of only 1 and 2 for Groups 2 and 3 workers respectively. This result indeed shows extreme dissatisfaction with this aspect of the job. Test of differences are accordingly significant at a 99.9 per cent confidence level between Groups 1 and 2 and between Groups 1 and 3 but not significant between Groups 2 and 3 workers (see Table 12).

Co-workers' behaviour was rated satisfactorily by Groups 1 and 2 workers with modal and median ratings of 5. However, Group 3 workers rated this aspect of job with dissatisfaction with a mean rating of less than 4. Accordingly, tests of differences were significant between Groups 1 and 3 and between Groups 2 and 3, but not between Groups 1 and 2 workers.

Similar to the rating of co-workers' behaviour, the physical conditions/working facilities which exist at universities were considered satisfactory by Groups 1 and 2 workers with modal and median ratings of 5. However, Group 3 workers rated this aspect of the job with dissatisfaction with modal and median value of 3 and a mean value of less than 3. Expectedly, tests of differences were significant between Groups 1 and 3 and between Groups 2 and 3, but not between the university teachers of Groups 1 and 2.

It is of interest to note and compare the mean scores of the three groups of workers with an estimate of how much of the time they feel satisfied with their job, their love or hatred for their job, their feelings about not changing their job, and how they compare with other workers on their likes or dislikes for their job. Table 11 shows that the mean scores of Group 1 workers were higher than those of Group 2, which were in turn higher than the mean scores of Group 3 workers for all these measures of comparison! This finding emphasises the difference between these groups of university teachers.

Implications of the groupings of university teachers

The results of the analyses show that a meaningful classification of university teachers, based on their job satisfaction profiles, is possible, despite the fact that university teachers vary widely in their job satisfaction levels for all aspects of their jobs.

The results from the cluster analysis shows there is an alternative way of classifying university teachers into distinct groups apart from the conventional classification based on job alone. Instead of using only one criterion—rank—the classification in this book is based on eight criteria incorporating aspects of the job for which the university teachers' satisfaction levels were recorded. The criteria employed sought to assess satisfaction with each of the following dimensions of their job: teaching, research, administration and management, present pay, promotions, supervision/-supervisor behaviour, co-workers' behaviour, and physical conditions/working facilities. A large set of relevant job criteria can clearly be used as a basis for clustering the academics into these three groups.

This grouping exercise also clearly shows that, overall a good percentage of the respondents (81%) are either happy or satisfied with their jobs. Therefore, the belief that UK academics may not be generally satisfied with their jobs (*Times Higher Education Supplement*, 1994, pp.1-2) seems to have been more widely publicised than well documented. Additionally, this grouping highlights that the productivity of 19 per cent of respondents whose productivity may perhaps be improved by addressing concerns that adversely affect their job satisfaction levels. These concerns are in the areas of pay, promotions and head of unit's supervision or behaviour.

Summary and conclusions

Workers, managers (Stewart, 1984, 1988) and academics (Oshagbemi, 1988) have been classified on the basis of characteristics, especially on how they spend their time.

This study has investigated the job satisfaction characteristics of UK academics. Using a cluster analytical methodology, it meaningfully classified university teachers into three groups 'happy workers' (Group 1), 'satisfied workers' (Group 2), and 'unhappy workers' (Group 3). It was found that happy and satisfied workers form a good percentage of the workforce in higher education. Nevertheless, the major characteristics of the job satisfaction profiles of unhappy workers were identified including their major concerns in the areas of pay, promotion, and head of unit's supervision or behaviour. If these concerns are properly addressed, the size and the gravity of the dissatisfaction experienced by unhappy workers may well be reduced.

Table 12 clearly defines the three groups of university teachers on the basis of major dimensions of the job examined. For example, the test of differences between happy and unhappy workers were not only significant on seven out of the eight tests examined, but also significant at a 99.9 per cent confidence level.

It must be reiterated that the grouping of university teachers was based on a sample of 554 UK university teachers who responded to the survey questionnaire. The naming of the groups should not be allowed to give the impression that there was complete uniformity within each category. It is emphasised that eight aspects of a university teacher's job were used for the classification, each aspect of a job was measured on a seven-point scale, and that only average data for the various groups were compared. It is possible, therefore, that a given university teacher in a group may not necessarily feature prominently in the criteria from which his/her group name was drawn.

Finally, absolute statements about the effectiveness of the three groups of university teachers cannot be made with certainty because the effectiveness of each group is relative. One problem when comparing the three groups is the difficulty of equating job satisfaction with effectiveness and productivity on the job. Obviously, such a link cannot be made directly or automatically. If job satisfaction levels were directly coterminous with productivity or effectiveness on the job, then Group 1 workers would be the most effective among the three groups. However, realising the high job satisfaction levels of Group 2 workers on teaching and research, careful interpretations have to be made. With this in mind it is interesting to note, that there were no significant differences between Groups 1 and 2 workers on the satisfaction levels derived from the primary functions of teaching and research. It may therefore be more reliable to say that workers in Groups 1 and 2 would tend to be more effective in their primary jobs when compared with Group 3 workers.

If administration and management is accepted as part of the university teacher's core functions, however, the situation becomes more complex. For this task, the job satisfaction levels (and possibly the effectiveness levels as well), of Group 1 workers would be greater than those of Group 3, which in turn would be greater than those of Group 2. If university goals were only teaching and research excellence, then Group 2 workers would probably be the most effective. But teaching and research functions cannot occur in isolation without an appropriate environment to carry them out, and this requirement emphasises the necessity for good administration and management.

CHAPTER 6

A Comparative Study of Academics and their Managers

Introduction

THIS CHAPTER INVESTIGATES WHETHER academics holding managerial jobs are, on the whole, more satisfied with their jobs than academics who do not hold similar administrative posts. Using a statistical test of differences, it was found that academics and their managers differ significantly in the levels of satisfaction derived from most aspects of their jobs. Sources of these differences are identified, and the general conclusion drawn is that a management job, characterised by seniority in age, rank, and length of service, positively affects university teachers' levels of job satisfaction.

Some research findings within the industrial sector suggest that managers tend to be more satisfied with their jobs when compared with other workers not occupying managerial jobs. The present study explores whether such general findings from industry are applicable in academia: whether there would be significant differences in the job satisfaction levels of academics and their managers. If the industrial situation is replicated in academia, the study will explore the reasons for the differences in the job satisfaction levels of academics and their managers. In particular, it will examine the socio-demographic characteristics and differences—age, length of service, rank and gender—of the two groups of workers in an attempt to explain the identified differences in their job satisfaction levels.

Literature review

As explained in Chapter 2, very few job satisfaction studies have been carried out within the university work environment. Furthermore, none of the reported studies seems to have researched the job satisfaction of academics and their managers. Unfortunately, even the industrial work environment does not seem to have many studies focused on managers and their workers.

Mottaz (1986) analysed data from 1,385 workers representing a variety of occupations. His findings suggest that overall satisfaction is positively related to occupational level: rank. He therefore concluded that it is useful to draw distinctions between workers in upper-level and lower-level occupations when attempting to make generalisations about workers' job satisfaction.

Forgionne and Peeters (1982) surveyed a random sample of 450 managers drawn from a variety of organisations in the USA. They found that the level of management, among other aspects, explained differences in job satisfaction. Similarly, Quinn et al. (1974) found that the job satisfaction of workers at managerial levels was higher than those of workers on the shopfloor.

In the UK, Oshagbemi (1997a) employed cluster analysis (Wishart, 1982, 1987) to classify university teachers into job satisfaction profiles but found no distinguishing characteristics among the three categories of workers in terms of the rank, leadership, or management responsibilities of the groups. However, Oshagbemi (1997b) has shown that rank and the interaction of rank and gender has a direct, positive and significant effect on the job satisfaction of university teachers. Similarly, Miles et al. (1996) found job level (rank) to be a significant predictor of workers' level of job satisfaction. Although publications on job satisfaction studies number in the thousands, and continue to grow in number, few of them seem to focus on the job satisfaction of workers and managers within a university work environment (Oshagbemi, 1999a).

The academics and their managers

To compare the job satisfaction of academics with that of their managers, we distinguish between the following groups in the total academic population, namely:

(1) Respondents who were head of department or division, dean of faculty, director of school, provost of college or institute, head of academic unit or centre. These are managers in their institutions and are designated as such.

(2) Respondents who indicated that they were not currently in charge of an academic unit or group. This group is simply called 'academics', 'the academics', or 'the other academics' as distinguished from managers. The group is analogous to the 'workers' category in private establishments or other employment sectors. It does not follow that this group does not have some administrative or managerial responsibilities, at least on an occasional, if not on a regular basis.

(3) Respondents who themselves indicated that they were in charge of an academic unit or group not indicated in (1) above. These are the year tutors or seminar co-ordinators who possibly carried out regular administrative assignments. This group can be regarded, in a sense, as 'supervisors' holding middle management jobs between managers and workers. There were 150 of the sampled academic staff members in this category. This finding shows that in addition to their teaching and research functions, university teachers also carry out significant administrative responsibilities.

The discussion in this section focuses on the similarities and differences between the first two groups: the academics and their managers.

The group designated as managers totalled 69, 46 males and 23 females, and comprised 14 lecturers, 22 senior lecturers, 6 readers, 25 professors, and 2 others. The average age was 54, and their average length of service in higher education was 20 years. The modal rank of this group was professor, whereas the median rank was senior lecturer. The mean rank was closer to reader than to senior lecturer.

Academics who indicated they did not currently hold administrative jobs totalled 347. Of this number, 211 were males and 136 were females. There were 219 lecturers, 100 senior lecturers, 13 readers, 13 professors, and 2 others. On average, their length of service in higher education was 15 years and their age was 48. In rank, their mean was closer to lecturer than senior lecturer whereas their modal and median rank was lecturer.

Similarities and differences in job satisfaction levels

Comparative data on academics and their managers are given in Table 13. This Table shows the percentages of academics and their managers who were satisfied with the various aspects of their jobs, the mean scores of the ratings of academics and their managers, on aspects of their jobs, and a significance test of differences between the mean scores of the academics and their managers.

Table 13: Comparison of academics and their managers on some aspects of their job satisfaction

Aspect of job	Percentage satisfied		Mean scores		t-value	Result
	Managers	Academics	Managers	Academics		
Teaching	89.5	75.6	5.49	4.98	3.59	p<0.001***
Co-workers' behaviour	79.7	68.8	5.12	4.78	2.20	p<0.05*
Research	64.2	64.6	4.79	4.63	0.70	NS
Physical conditions/	64.0	49.4	4.72	4.04	3.27	p<0.01**
working facilities	64.8	57.0	4.69	4.29	2.08	p<0.05*
Head of units' supervision	48.6	38.3	4.25	3.91	1.77	NS
Administration and	44.6	24.2	4.05	3.28	3.83	p<0.001***
management	33.8	28.8	3.52	3.40	0.53	NS
Promotion						
Present pay						

* = significant at 95% confidence level; ** = significant at 99% confidence level; *** significant at 99.9% confidence level.

From Table 13, it can be clearly seen that, without exception, the mean scores recorded by the managers were higher than the corresponding mean scores recorded by the other academics on all aspects of their jobs. Similarly, with one very minor exception, the percentages of the academics who were satisfied with all aspects of their jobs were lower than the corresponding percentages of the managers who were satisfied with various aspects of their jobs.

One conclusion from Table 13, therefore, is that, in general, academics are less satisfied with their jobs than are their managers. Stated differently, managers in academic institutions, such as the director of a school, or the head of an academic department, are more satisfied with their jobs than the other academics who do not hold similar or comparable managerial jobs. It is, however, useful to examine the test of statistical differences provided on Table 13 to see the aspects of their job where the recorded differences between the academics and their managers are significant.

Table 13 shows that there are five out of eight aspects of the university teachers' job, where significant statistical differences exist between the mean scores of the academics and their managers. It is interesting to note that managers in academic institutions derive more satisfaction from teaching than the other academics, although it is probable that the managers do not teach for as many hours as other academics. The explanation is perhaps that, over the years, managers in academic institutions have taught for a longer period of time and have acquired greater teaching skills and experience that enables them to derive greater job satisfaction from teaching. Or perhaps they teach at a different level, for example postgraduate or final year undergraduate as opposed to the earlier years.

Managers also derive more satisfaction from promotions in their various institutions as compared with the other academics. This finding is unsurprising. Most managers in academic institutions are professors and readers who have benefited from the promotion processes, and they would, therefore, be expected to derive a great deal of job satisfaction from that aspect of their job. In fact, our data reveal that compared with managers, the percentage of the other academics who were satisfied with their promotions was slightly more than half.

In respect of the head of units' supervision, significant statistical differences also exist in the comparison of academics and their managers in the level of their satisfaction on this aspect of their job. Actually, the managers, who by virtue of their jobs experience the problems of leadership would, perhaps, tend to be more sympathetic to, and therefore satisfied with the supervision of other managers.

This explanation may also account for the significantly higher job satisfaction that managers derive from their physical conditions/ working facilities in their institutions when compared to the feeling of other academics. Managers plan the operational details of their units, execute their budgets, and manage their staff, among other responsibilities. Exposure to the practical realities of meeting objectives, realising targets, motivating staff may have beneficial effects in assisting managers to better appreciate realities. Such an appreciation may increase the level of job satisfaction that they derive from their physical conditions/working facilities. Alternatively, it could be argued that the managers enjoy the privileges of their appointments—for example, big offices and control of organisational affairs.

Job satisfaction derived from co-workers' behaviour is the other aspect of their job where significant differences existed between the mean scores of the managers in academic institutions and other academics. Managers in academic institutions, perhaps like other managers, depend very much on their co-workers' co-operation and positive attitudes to get their units' function accomplished. Because managers in academia generally get co-operation from most of their colleagues, it is hypothesised that this aspect of their job would tend to give them more job satisfaction as compared with the other academics who do not hold similar managerial posts. It must be pointed out that, although there is some measure of interdependence in performing academic responsibilities as a whole, some academics who are not managers may and do exhibit some level of independence in executing their functions. Such academics may, therefore, not derive as much job satisfaction from colleagues' co-operation as a manager would. Academics as a group tend to be individuals rather than team players and so may not fully co-operate.

There were three aspects of their jobs where the statistical test of differences between the mean scores of the academics and their managers did not prove significant:—research, present pay, and administration and management.

It is interesting to note that the managers in academia did not derive significantly greater satisfaction from research than other academics. This is of interest because it was success at research activity, in many cases, which saw them elected or appointed as managers in the first instance. However, as managers, many people no longer have the time for research activities and therefore, their level of satisfaction from research may be lower than what it was before they became managers. This is because they perform fewer research activities as managers, and they enjoy fewer of the tangible and intangible benefits of research.

It is not suggested, however, that managers in academic institutions are necessarily better researchers than other academics who may not hold managerial posts. In fact, some academics, if they can avoid it, would not accept a management or a leadership job because of their commitment to research excellence. In an earlier study, Oshagbemi (1988, pp.164-165), found that British managers in academic institutions were not particularly motivated towards management and that many of them accepted their management jobs as the cost of holding chairs. This tendency is explained by Etzioni (1964, p.83) who states that, most successful professionals are not motivated to become administrators, and that it is those who feel that they have little chance of becoming outstanding professionals in their fields who tend to gravitate towards administrative and managerial jobs.

Academics who were not currently holding management jobs, did not derive a greater level of satisfaction from research compared with their managers. What seems significant is that the mean scores from this aspect of their jobs were relatively high for both groups, signifying that academics and their managers derive a high level of satisfaction from research.

There was no significant difference between the mean scores of the academics and their managers on their present pay. Both groups of workers were about equally dissatisfied with this aspect of their jobs. Unlike private industries, holding managerial posts within academia is not well remunerated. The allowances often attached to these posts are really very small compared with the responsibilities that office holders are asked to shoulder. Perhaps, this is why, in the past, or in some universities, one of the costs of holding a chair is assuming administrative responsibilities for the particular academic unit!

It may be instructive to know that some universities are reportedly appointing professional managers and subordinating professors under them (Eggins, 1994, p.3). Yet, there are some management tasks, such as postgraduate admissions, the management of research activity, and the recruitment of senior academics, which appear best performed by academics. It would therefore appear that, in many cases, what may be required is management training for managers in academic institutions instead of side-lining them.

Both academics and their managers did not rate the satisfaction derived from administration and management highly and there was no significant difference in the mean scores on that aspect of their jobs. Perhaps, more people should be allowed to indicate their interest in managerial posts rather than thrusting such posts on professors as the cost of holding chairs. If appointment of managers in academic institutions on the basis of expressed individual choice and suitability were the general practice, then perhaps more managers would derive significantly greater satisfaction from performing the task they like when compared with other academics.

This may be the case especially if the managers in academic institutions espouse management training designed to increase their productivity and effectiveness on this task. At present, this does not seem to be the case. However, even when some academics volunteer to take on some administrative responsibilities, one is not sure whether they are doing such jobs because they are interested or because they want to boost their salaries with which they are dissatisfied.

It is illuminating to explore the reasons for the differences in the level of job satisfaction between academics and their managers, as in Table 13. The socio-demographic characteristics of the two groups were closely examined, and the following found:

- Length of service in higher education—managers had served, on average, for 20 years whereas other academics had only served, on average, for 15 years. This difference was statistically significant at the $p < 0.001$ level.

- Age—the age of managers was, on average, 54 years, whereas other academics, were, on average, 48 years old. Again, this difference was significant at the $p < 0.001$ level.

- Gender—there was no significant difference in the proportion of males/females in the two groups. In the managers group, the proportion of females was 0.33333 whereas the corresponding figure for other academics was 0.39193.

- Rank—the modal rank in the group of the managers was professor, whereas the modal rank in the other group was lecturer. The difference in rank was significant at the $p < 0.001$ level.

Managers in academic institutions, therefore, seem to be a sub-group of their own with differences in their age, rank, length of service in higher education, and management job, when compared with other academics. It is therefore concluded that management job, characterised by seniority in age, rank, and length of service, affects university teachers' level of job satisfaction positively. This conclusion is consistent with other research findings, (Quinn et al., 1974, p.9; Forgionne and Peters, 1982, p.104; Mottaz, 1986, p.364) which suggests that managers, on the whole, tend to enjoy greater job satisfaction than workers.

It must be stated that, so far, the analyses have only established that the socio-demographic factors identified together affect the level of a worker's job satisfaction. It is still necessary and useful to establish whether these factors, individually, constitute important determinants of job satisfaction, at least within academia. For example, in earlier research, it was found that rank has a direct, positive and significant effect on the job satisfaction of university teachers (Oshagbemi, 1997b). In addition, although gender, on its own, is not significantly related to job satisfaction, it is significant when compared to the rank of university teachers.

It is observed that age, length of service in the organisation, and seniority or rank, are three time-related concepts associated with job satisfaction (Ronen, 1978; Mottaz, 1987; Eichar et al., 1991; Orpen, 1995; Miles et al., 1996; Tamayo, 1996). This study of academics and their managers has shown, at least, a group relevance of the variables in affecting the level of job satisfaction.

Summary and conclusions of the comparative study

The results of the survey show that managers in universities exhibit similar characteristics to other academics in the satisfaction or dissatisfaction derived from some aspects of their jobs. The aspects of their jobs where there were no significant differences between the mean scores of the academics and their managers are: administration and management, research, and present pay.

By contrast, the two groups showed significant differences in the level of job satisfaction derived from the following aspects of their jobs: teaching, co-workers' behaviour, head of units' behaviour, physical conditions/working facilities, and promotions. Without exception, the mean scores obtained by managers in all aspects of their jobs were higher than the mean scores in the corresponding aspects of other academics' jobs. Because significant differences exist in the majority of these mean differences, it is concluded that, overall, managers in academic institutions derive greater job satisfaction from their jobs than do other academics. Even when academics and their managers were both dissatisfied with aspects of their jobs, such as present pay, managers were less dissatisfied compared to other academics.

In offering possible explanations for the results of the research, it is important to note that the observed differences between managers and other academics are not because managers perform administration and management or engage in any other specific task, but because of the characteristics of the group as a whole. In fact, it will be recalled that in this study, there were no significant differences between the academics and their managers on satisfaction enjoyed from administrative and managerial responsibilities.

An implication of these findings is that, because managers in academia are significantly different from other academics in a number of areas, it is useful for universities to continue to involve academic groups such as school boards or departments in major policy or organisational decisions, instead of relying totally on suggestions from their managers. This means that academic policy in higher education should continue to be democratised and academics should continue to be given opportunity and respect for their very useful inputs into the decision-making processes in universities. In this way academic policies and practices would tend to reflect the views of the academia as a whole and not just the views of their managers who seem to be a group that differs from other academics.

CHAPTER 7

Age and Job Satisfaction

Introduction

THIS CHAPTER CONCENTRATES ON the relationship between age and job satisfaction. It notes that in today's organisations a general trend is for staffing by older workers. An interesting question, therefore, is whether older workers are more satisfied with their jobs when compared to younger employees? An objective of this study is to investigate the effects of age on the job satisfaction of UK academics. Using frequency analysis, the overall job satisfaction score of the academics was positively related to age. A three-way analysis of variance (ANOVA) confirmed the hypothesis that age is linearly related to the overall measure of job satisfaction. Further analyses show that the age of academics is significantly related to their satisfaction with teaching, research, and administration and management: the core aspects of their job. The nature of the relationship is explored. It is observed that the construct developed for ascertaining an overall measure of job satisfaction was more rigorous than the popular Job Descriptive Index.

Arising from the post–Second World War baby boom, many countries are currently facing the problem of an ageing population. This problem is manifested, for example, in a change to the age composition of the work-force. The UK is no exception to the general trend of organisations staffed with older workers: a similar trend was reported in Singapore (Kong, et al., 1993) and the USA (Eichar, et al., 1991).

A recent publication by the Government Statistical Service confirms that UK has an ageing population (Church, 1994, p.2). For example, the number of people over pensionable age is projected to exceed 16 million by 2031 which is—more than double the number in 1961 (Church, 1994, p.21). Table 14 presents a distribution of the percentage of the population who were 80 years or over in 1961, 1971, 1981 and 1991 and it also gives projections for 2001, 2011, and 2021 (Church, 1994, p.23). From the table, it is clear that the percentage of people of at least 80 years of age increased steadily from 1961 to 1991. In addition, the projections show a further increase in the percentage of senior citizens.

It is noted that although there has been a decline in the birth rate in the UK, the overall population is growing steadily. Clearly the number of births each year exceeds the number of deaths. The average age of the UK population is increasing for two reasons. Firstly, with a slow-down in the birth rate, there are fewer young people to decrease the average age of the population. Secondly, life expectancy is increasing, and an increase in the number of older people raises the average age.

A breakdown of respondents to this study (Table 15) shows that over 50 per cent are at least 45 years old with some 86 per cent at least 35 years of age. There are no data to substantiate or refute the statement that the academic population in the UK is also ageing. However, even if the overall academic population is growing steadily older, the satisfaction of academics with their jobs may not be improving (Oshagbemi, 1996). This study investigates the impact of age on the job satisfaction of university teachers in the UK, and addresses the question of whether age or age and interaction with gender and/or rank is related to job satisfaction. In essence, this chapter examines the relationship between age and the job satisfaction of academics (Oshagbemi, 1998; Hickson and Oshagbemi, 1999).

This study also discusses academics' overall job satisfaction and their satisfaction with teaching, research and administration and managerial duties. As also suggested by Abu-Saad and Hendrix (1995), in the current sample teachers' satisfaction with the work itself—teaching, research, and administration and management, is the dominant job satisfaction factor.

Table 14: UK population

Year	Population (million)	Population 80+ years (%)
1961	52.8	1.9
1971	55.9	2.3
1981	56.4	2.8
1991	57.8	3. 7
2001	59.7	4.2
2011	61.1	4.7
2021	62.0	5.2

Source: Church (1994, p.23)

Literature review

Labour market trends indicate that older workers may come to play an increasingly important role in the work force (Eichar, et al., 1991, p.609), and the work orientation of this group of employees is therefore of both theoretical and practical interest. A review of the relevant literature shows that most age–job satisfaction studies conclude that there is some association between employee age and job satisfaction.

Gibson and Klein (1970) found an increase in satisfaction with age over all tenure levels in their sample of university teachers. They explained the age-satisfaction relationship in terms of changing needs, a mellowing process, and changing cognitive structures associated with age. From their studies, Siassi et al. (1975) reported higher levels of job satisfaction in workers over 40 than in under 40 workers, regardless of length of service. They explained this result by suggesting an increase in coping capacity with age, perhaps as a result of greater stability, ego strength and similar factors.

Glenn et al. (1977) suggest that cohort differences may play a part in the age–job relationship, in particular the tendency for older workers to have had less formal education than young adults. Their theory suggests that education has a negative impact on job satisfaction because increased education is associated with higher expectations, and a person may become dissatisfied with performing the routine tasks required of most jobs. Wright and Hamilton (1978) offer evidence supporting the job change hypothesis as an explanation for the age-satisfaction relationship. They state that virtually all the evidence is consistent with the hypothesis that older workers are more satisfied than younger workers only because they have better jobs, where 'better' is defined in terms of what people themselves think is important in their work.

Ronen (1978) reported a linear relationship between age and job satisfaction in a sample of private-sector production workers but not in a sample of Israeli kibbutz workers. Near et al. (1978) examined the relationship between age, occupational level and overall satisfaction, reporting that the strongest predictors of job satisfaction among 18 variables were occupational level and age. When the effects of occupational level were controlled, age remained a significant predictor of satisfaction. O'Brien and Dowling (1981) reported similar findings to those of Glenn et al (1977). O'Brien and Dowling investigated variables representing ageing effects including skill utilisation, measure of influence and income in addition to education. They found that neither cohort nor ageing variables alone account for the positive association between age and job satisfaction, but rather that it was a result of both cohort and ageing effects, and specifically the decreasing difference between perceived and desired attributes.

In his review and analysis Rhodes (1983) concluded that job satisfaction was positively and linearly associated with age. Rhodes arrived at this conclusion after a review of the findings of seven other separate studies (Aldag, and Brief, 1975; Siassi, et al., 1975; Stagner, 1975; Ronen, 1978; Near, et al., 1978; Weaver, 1978; Staines, and Quinn, 1979). Similarly, Doering et al.'s (1983) comprehensive review concluded that age is positively associated with job satisfaction.

Many studies have sought to explain age variations in job satisfaction. Mottaz (1987) listed four possible explanations to account for such variations.

1. Firstly, he suggested that cohort differences may have an influence, because younger workers attach significantly greater importance to intrinsic rewards, like interesting and challenging jobs, compared to older workers who are more concerned with extrinsic rewards such as pay and fringe benefits. Hence younger workers are more dissatisfied than older workers simply because they demand more than their jobs can provide.

2. Secondly, he suggested that there was an influence from job change. Older workers possess more seniority and work experience, which enable them to move easily into more rewarding and satisfying jobs.

3. Thirdly, 'grinding down' was suggested as an explanation. Older workers consider rewards like interesting work, autonomy or promotion as less important and more difficult to attain, and hence they demand less from their jobs and are more satisfied with their work than younger people.

4. Finally, the theory of accommodation was suggested. After staying in their jobs for some time, workers tend to adjust their work values to the conditions of the work place, resulting in greater job satisfaction.

However, in an empirical study by Luthans and Thomas (1989) the nature of the relationship between age and job satisfaction was found to be curvilinear rather than linear as in the findings of earlier researchers. Luthans and Thomas offered three explanations for the lower level of job satisfaction for their sample after the age of 40.

1. It may be due to the process of accommodation and resignation in that older workers may become increasingly disappointed, recognising that their expectations and aspirations are becoming more and more limited.
2. The reason may be bound up with an individual's attempt to cope with the idea of earlier retirement. A worker may experience an increase in job stress and feel that his or her job is not as satisfying as it used to be, in an attempt to justify retiring early.
3. Older worker may experience increased pressure from factors such as changing technologies, role overload or an increasing emphasis on objective productivity measures.

Kong et al. (1993) examined the effects of age on the level of job satisfaction of accountants in Singapore. Their results show that there is generally a positive association between age and job satisfaction. In addition the investigators found an interaction between age and job type. This finding may partially explain whether the relationship between age and job satisfaction is linear or curvilinear, because the relationship detected may be a function of the type, (i.e. the sample investigated). More recently, Clark et al. (1996) investigated the relation between job satisfaction and age, using survey responses from a large sample of British employees. Their paper provides strong evidence for a U-shaped relationship between age and job satisfaction. The importance of changed expectations with increasing age is emphasised.

To date, therefore, there seems to be extensive evidence of a relationship between employee age and job satisfaction. However, the nature of this relationship, whether linear or curvilinear, remains unclear. Results obtained from empirical investigations are, perhaps, in part, a function of the occupational group examined. This study investigates the relationship between age and job satisfaction among university teachers, a group of people who conduct research studies a lot but are themselves seldom researched!

Statistical methods

To study the effect of age on the job satisfaction of university teachers, while allowing for gender and rank, a three-way ANOVA, was performed. The direct effects of age, gender, and rank, and all interactive effects among age, gender, and rank, were investigated. Not only is overall job satisfaction in relation to age investigated, but also satisfaction with research, teaching, and administration and management in relation to age. Descriptive statistics were also computed to examine the overall job satisfaction levels across the different classifications of university teachers. In addition, histograms showing the nature of the relationship between age and overall satisfaction, and between age and satisfaction with teaching, research, and administration and management, are presented to depict the nature of the relationships graphically.

Table 15: Breakdown of respondents by age, gender and rank

	Frequency	%	Overall job satisfaction score
Age			
Under 35	79	14.3	4.173
35 to 44	194	35.0	4.196
45 to 54	204	36.8	4.208
At least 55	77	13.9	4.290
Gender			
Male	337	60.8	4.206
Female	217	39.2	4.220

Rank			
Lecturer	306	55.2	4.118
Senior lecturer	175	31.6	4.283
Reader	25	4.5	4.327
Professor	48	8.7	4.484

Note Overall job satisfaction score for all respondents: 4.212. Standard deviation: 0.798.

Results and discussion

From Table 15, when age is considered in isolation, the overall job satisfaction score is lowest for university teachers of less than 35 years of age (overall job satisfaction score 4.173). Satisfaction increases progressively for each older age group, with a final satisfaction score of 4.290 for university teachers aged 55 or older. This indicates that older university teachers are generally more satisfied with the job than their younger counterparts. The age of university teachers seems thus to be related to their level of job satisfaction. Table 15 also shows that female university teachers are generally more satisfied with their jobs, with an overall job satisfaction score of 4.220, compared with male university teachers whose overall job satisfaction score is 4.206.

Further, by classifying university teachers according to their rank, Table 15 shows that lecturers are least satisfied with their jobs, with an overall job satisfaction score of 4.118, followed by senior lecturers (4.283), readers (4.327), and professors were the most satisfied, with an overall job satisfaction score of 4.484.

Another breakdown of the overall job satisfaction scores of the ranks of university teachers by age group and by gender is given in Table 16. Although difficult to extract findings from the three-way cross-tabulation, it is clear that no university teacher, male or female, below 35 years of age, was a reader or a professor. Could this suggest an ageing academic population, or that the age of academics tends to be higher than that of workers in other employment sectors? It is interesting to note that no female university teacher in the sample was a reader, but three female professors record overall satisfaction scores much higher than the average for the sample. Does this suggest that female professors of all ages are happier than their male counterparts?

Table 16: Overall job satisfaction score, by age and gender

Age	Lecturers	Senior lecturers	Readers	Professors	All types
Male academics					
Less than 35	4.169	4.031	----	----	4.155
35 to 44	4.108	4.168	3.938	4.458	4.138
45 to 54	4.215	4.228	4.250	4.357	4.249
At least 55	3.941	4.429	4.563	4.513	4.285
All age groups	4.133	4.245	4.213	4.416	4.206
Female academics					
Less than 35	4.188	4.188	----	----	4.193
35 to 44	4.253	4.212	----	5.750★	4.275
45 to 54	3.781	4.425	----	5.125★	4.129
At least 55	4.016	4.422	----	5.125★	4.272
All age groups	4.091	4.338	----	5.333	4.220

Note ★ Only one valid case; ---- no responses in this category.

Figure 1 shows a histogram of frequency analyses depicting the nature of the relationship between age and overall job satisfaction and between age and satisfaction with teaching, research, and administration and management. This figure shows, consistent with the information from Table 15, that level of overall job satisfaction score increases proportionately with age, suggesting a positive linear model of overall job satisfaction. This indicates that, in general, the older an academic is, the more satisfied he or she tends to be with his or her job as a whole. However, this tentative finding needs to be tested for statistical significance: whether the differences in age groups in relation to job satisfaction levels are significant.

Age	Overall job satisfaction	Teaching satisfaction	Research satisfaction	Satisfaction with administration and management
Less than 35	4.173	5.051	5.013	3.91
35 to < 44	4.196	4.85	4.684	3.705
45 to < 54	4.208	4.995	4.475	4.025
At least 55	4.29	5.468	4.156	3.896

Figure 1: Histograms showing the nature of relationships between age and overall satisfaction and between age and satisfaction with teaching, research and administration and management

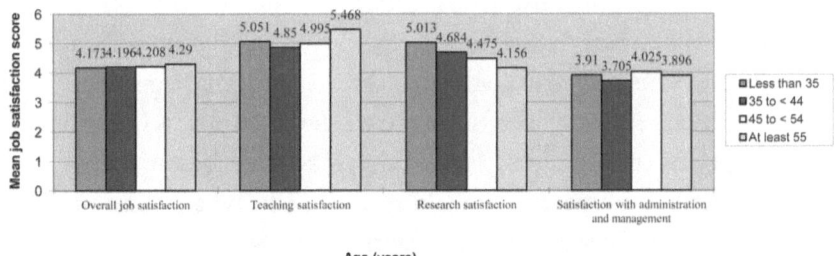

Younger academics, less than 35 years of age, are more satisfied with teaching when compared with some older academics. This initial satisfaction level may be explained by the enthusiasm of new entrants into a profession. However, the happiness of university teachers with teaching reduces by the time they are in the 35 to 44 age range. This is a phase when academics seem to better appraise and appreciate the realities of this aspect of their jobs. As they grow older, until retirement age, their level of satisfaction with teaching increases, perhaps as a result of their more skilful approach to the task and their better consequent performance.

The finding for research satisfaction, which consistently decreased with age, was rather surprising. The explanation may lie in the probability that older academics will not execute many new research projects, but may well be supervising research students and writing papers on previous research. Another possible explanation is that, over the years, the method for funding research projects has changed dramatically. Unlike earlier years, when 'blue skies' research was encouraged, applied research currently receives most financial support from funding bodies. Thus the satisfaction, derived from initiating and executing new research projects, may have declined in higher education. Over time, opportunities for promotion have also reduced *vis-à-vis* eligible applicants. Some eligible lecturers do not have vacant professorial positions they can aspire to, and this consideration possibly gives rise to dissatisfaction with success in research as a means of helping them obtain a Chair.

Satisfaction with administration and management does not follow a consistent pattern relative to age, as shown in Figure 1. Academics seem to be satisfied with administration and management when under 35 years of age: the satisfaction level drops when they are about 40, only to rise again some ten years later, but it finally drops towards retirement age. Age would not seem to be a strong predictor of a consistent satisfaction pattern with this task.

Advanced statistical analysis is especially helpful in throwing light on the frequency analysis discussed above. Table 17 gives ANOVA results which show that, for overall job satisfaction, age, and interactions of age with rank and/or gender, are not statistically significant. This indicates that the tentative interpretation of the results of the frequency analysis—that overall job satisfaction increases with age—is not supported by a more rigorous statistical analysis. In essence, this means, that for all ages, the level of job satisfaction is similar, confirming a linear function for overall job satisfaction. However, rank and the interaction of rank and gender are statistically significant in predicting overall job satisfaction (see Table 17). As overall job satisfaction does not significantly increase proportionate to age, a positive linear relationship between job satisfaction and age is assumed. This shows that, although there are differences in overall job satisfaction levels among different age groups, as revealed by the frequency analysis, the differences are not statistically significant.

Table 17 also shows that, for research and teaching satisfaction, age and the interaction of age and rank, and the interaction of age, rank, and gender, are statistically significant. This indicates that age explains satisfaction with teaching and research and that the interaction of age with rank and with rank and gender also explains satisfaction in these core aspects of a university teachers' job. The degree of confidence in this explanation is provided by the individual F values. The nature of the satisfaction in these considerations is presented graphically in Figure 1. From the histogram, the older an academic is, the less satisfaction he or she derives from research, whereas, with the exception of academics under 35, the older an academic, the more satisfaction he or she derives from teaching.

The interaction of age and gender is also significant with respect to teaching satisfaction but not to research. This indicates that, although gender by itself is not significantly related to teaching satisfaction, it is significant when compared with the age of university teachers. The nature of the relationship is a matter for further analysis. With respect to administration and management, age, the interaction of age and gender, and the interaction of age, gender, and rank, are all statistically significant. Table 17 gives the level of statistical significance in each case. This shows that age and the various interactions of age with gender and rank are significant predictors of satisfaction levels in the task of administration and management.

Table 17: ANOVA results: overall[1] job satisfaction and satisfaction with research, teaching, and administration and management

Aspect of job:		Overall job		Research		Teaching		Administration and management	
Source:	df	F value	Pr > F	F value	Pr > F	F value	Pr > F	F value	Pr > F
Age	4	0.228	0.923	2.389	0.050**	4.485	0.001***	2.309	0.057*
Gender	1	0.037	0.848	0.002	0.961	1.035	0.309	0.733	0.392
Rank	4	2.925	0.021	5.626	0.000	1.368	0.244	0.120	0.975
Age x gender	6	0.453	0.843	1.888	0.802	2.827	0.010***	2.102	0.052*
Rank x gender	6	2.976	0.012	3.178	0.005	1.036	0.401	0.412	0.871
Age x rank	7	0.791	0.595	4.686	0.000***	3.209	0.003***	1.562	0.145
Age x rank x gender	7	0.575	0.776	3.168	0.003***	1.963	0.059*	2.058	0.047**

Notes *= $p < 0.10$; ** = $p \leq 0.05$; *** = $p \leq 0.01$. Overall[1] job satisfaction was defined as the mean of the summation of the individual job satisfaction measures: satisfaction levels in (teaching + research + administration and management + present pay + promotions + head of unit's supervision + co-workers' behaviour + physical conditions/working facilities)/8.

Results presented in Table 17 show clearly that, whereas age alone does not predict overall job satisfaction of academics, age seems to be significantly related to satisfaction levels in their main tasks of teaching, research, and administration and management. Unfortunately the pattern of relationships between age and satisfaction in teaching and between age and satisfaction in administration and management is not clear. There is, however, a clear negative relationship between age and satisfaction with research. The nature of the relationships between age and satisfaction in each of these tasks is presented in Figure 1. The interaction of age with gender and rank shows consistent significant results in this dimension of the three tasks, as detailed in Table 17.

Summary, conclusions and implications

This study examines the effects of age on the level of job satisfaction of UK academics. The model used to test overall job satisfaction summarises satisfaction levels in eight aspects of the university teacher's job, namely teaching, research, administration and management, present pay, opportunities for promotion, supervision/supervisor behaviour, co-workers behaviour, and physical conditions/working facilities. Thus, the construct is more rigorous than the popular Job Descriptive Index, which uses five aspects of a job in its formulation (Smith, et al., 1969, 1975, 1985).

The frequency analyses indicate there is a linear and positive association between age and overall job satisfaction, as found in the literature (see for example, Hulin and Smith, 1964, 1965; Doering et al., 1983; Rhodes, 1983; Lee and Wilbur, 1985). Older employees may be better able to adjust their expectations to the rewards that work can provide. Additionally, older workers may gain esteem simply by virtue of the length of time spent in the job (DeSantis and Durst, 1996). Clark et al. (1996 p.77) explain that older workers are more satisfied, not only because they tend to be better rewarded, but also because they expect less or they care less about the reward from their job. Other proposed explanations argue that older workers are more satisfied than their younger counterparts because they actually have 'better' or more highly rewarded jobs (Quinn et al., 1974; Wright and Hamilton, 1978). However, the results of a three-way ANOVA carried out in this study, did not confirm a significant relationship between age and overall job satisfaction. A positive linear relationship between age and overall job satisfaction, which was found in the frequency analyses, is therefore assumed.

The results of three-way ANOVA showed that significant associations exist between age and satisfaction in teaching, research, and administration and management—the basic aspects of academics work. The nature of these relationships is discussed with reference to

Figure 1. Satisfaction levels in the other five aspects of the construct of the university teacher's job were not tested here for significance.

The ANOVA results also confirm that the interaction of age and gender, of age and rank, and of age, rank, and gender, reaches statistically significant satisfaction levels in the research, teaching, and administration and management aspects of an academic's job. The findings, therefore, reveal that age is related to satisfaction levels in the core aspects of the university teachers' job. Whereas the nature of the impact of age on the job satisfaction of academics varies from one aspect of the job to another (see Figure 1), the nature of overall job satisfaction to age seems to be linear. It is of interest to note that satisfaction levels, with the main tasks of university teachers, (i.e. teaching, research, and administration and management, in relation to age), are statistically significant: age does affect the level of satisfaction derived from performing these tasks. With the exception of research, however, the nature of the relationship between age and the other two tasks is not clear.

Indeed, the findings of this study suggest that more research is needed to confirm the nature of the relationship, if any, between overall job satisfaction and the age of university academics. Such research could also further explore the nature of the relationship between age and satisfaction in research, teaching, or administration and management. If a negative relationship between age and satisfaction in research, which was found in this study, is confirmed by future studies, it may well signal a need to review educational policies regarding available professorial posts with a view to creating vacancies for deserving professorial aspirants. The need for funding bodies to encourage generic or 'blue skies' research, and not just applied research, may also be a consideration. Such a policy decision would not only increase the satisfaction of talented researchers, it would also encourage greater innovation in societal activities generally, and lead to a review of the funding of research projects in UK universities. As a possible direction for future research, more extensive studies could be carried out to examine other factors that affect the level of job satisfaction of academics in universities.

CHAPTER 8

Rank and Job Satisfaction

Introduction

IS THERE ANY ASSOCIATION between an individual's rank and the level of his or her job satisfaction? This chapter investigates the answers to this question as it pertains to UK academics. Results indicate that rank has a direct, positive and significant effect on the job satisfaction of university teachers, but that age and gender do not. Lecturers are the least satisfied with their jobs followed by senior lecturers, readers and professors in this order. In addition, the interactive effect between rank and gender on job satisfaction is statistically significant. This means that although gender by itself is not significantly related to job satisfaction, it is significant when compared with the rank of university teachers. Female academics at higher ranks, namely, senior lecturers, readers and professors, are more satisfied with their jobs than male academics of comparable ranks. Further analyses show that rank by itself and the interactive effect between rank and gender are significantly related to satisfaction with pay, promotion, and physical conditions/working facilities at UK universities.

Literature review

Rank, as used in this book, refers to an individual's job status in an organisation: it indicates an employee's job level or job seniority in a particular occupational classification. Within the context of UK universities, it indicates whether an academic worker is a lecturer, senior lecturer, reader, or a professor. The primary question addressed is whether rank affects an academic's level of job satisfaction and, if so, how? Other issues explored are the individual relationships between pay, promotion, physical conditions/working facilities and job satisfaction in UK universities.

Research studies designed to investigate whether job satisfaction increases with higher rank are relatively few. A search of relevant articles through the Institute of Scientific Information Social Sciences Database revealed only 23 articles published between 1981 and 1997, inclusive. The search used 'occupational level', 'job level', and 'job rank' as keywords in titles. Thirteen, seven, and three successful records respectively were obtained for these words during the title search period. Ronen (1978) noted that job satisfaction increased with occupational level. Near et al. (1978) examined the relationship between age, occupational level and overall satisfaction, reporting that the strongest predictors of job satisfaction among 18 variables were occupational levels, (i.e. rank and age).

Miles et al. (1996) found job level (rank) to be a significant predictor of workers' level of job satisfaction. They examined job level as a structural determinant of role behaviour and suggest that the job level moderated the communication–job satisfaction relationship. Grimes and Register (1997) examined career publications and academic job rank from a sample of 102 economists who received PhD's in 1968 and were subsequently employed by a US institution of higher learning. The result indicates, as expected, that publishing is positively correlated to job rank. However, the research did not attempt to establish a relationship between job rank and job satisfaction.

Holden and Black (1996) surveyed a random sample of 293 psychologists employed as faculty members in medical schools to evaluate professional activities, academic productivity and work satisfaction. Clear differences in productivity and satisfaction by academic rank were found. Full professors displayed higher levels of productivity and satisfaction than associate or assistant professors.

Evidence from literature seems to suggest that rank is a reliable predictor of job satisfaction, with workers at higher ranks being generally more satisfied with their jobs compared with workers at lower ranks. The aim of this chapter is to examine the influence of rank on the job satisfaction of UK academics (Oshagbemi, 1997b).

Statistical methods

To study the effect of rank on the job satisfaction of university teachers, at the same time allowing for age and gender, a three-way analysis of variance, (ANOVA), was performed. The direct effects of rank, age, and gender, and all interactive effects between rank, age, and gender, were investigated. Investigations included not only overall job satisfaction in relation to rank, but also satisfaction with present pay, promotions and with the physical conditions/ working facilities that exist in their organisations in relation to rank. Descriptive statistics were also computed to examine the overall job satisfaction levels across the different classifications of university teachers. In addition, histograms showing the nature of the relationship between rank and overall satisfaction, and between rank and satisfaction with present pay, promotion, and the physical conditions/working facilities which exist in their organisations were presented to depict the nature of these relationships graphically. Table 18 gives a breakdown of respondents by rank, age and gender.

Results and discussion

Table 18 presents the ANOVA results which show that, for the direct effects and a 0.05 significance level, gender and age are not statistically significant, but rank is, with a p-value of 0.021. This implies that the job satisfaction of university teachers is significantly dependent on rank but not on age or gender. It must be noted that, although gender by itself is not statistically significant, the interactive effect of rank and gender is significant ($p<0.012$). This means that although gender by itself is not significantly related to job satisfaction, it is significant when compared together with the rank of university teachers. All other interactive effects are not statistically significant with respect to overall job satisfaction.

Table 18: ANOVA results: overall[1] job satisfaction and satisfaction with present pay, promotion, and physical conditions/working facilities

Aspect of job:		Overall job		Present pay		Promotion		Physical conditions/ working facilities	
Source:	df	F value	Pr > F	F value	Pr > F	F value	Pr > F	F value	Pr > F
Age	4	0.228	0.923	1.095	0.358	0.437	0.782	1.577	0.179
Gender	1	0.037	0.848	7.634	0.006	0.091	0.763	4.634	0.032
Rank	4	2.925	0.021**	6.378	0.000***	23.699	0.000***	2.198	0.068*
Gender x age	6	0.453	0.843	2.927	0.008	0.868	0.518	1.443	0.196
Rank x gender	6	2.976	0.012**	3.938	0.001***	12.697	0.000***	2.077	0.054*
Rank x age	7	0.791	0.595	2.920	0.005***	6.622	0.000***	1.570	0.142
Rank x gender x age	7	0.575	0.776	1.668	0.115	1.442	0.187	1.935	0.063*

Notes *= $p < 0.10$; ** = $p < 0.05$; *** = $p < 0.01$. Overall[1] job satisfaction was defined as the mean of the summation of the individual job satisfaction measures: satisfaction levels in (teaching + research + administration and management + present pay + promotion + head of unit's supervision + co-workers' behaviour + physical conditions/working facilities)/8.

ANOVA results of the interactive effects of rank and gender are presented graphically in Figure 2. From this histogram, both male and female lecturers are almost equally satisfied with their jobs, although female academics experience higher satisfaction levels than their male counterparts for the ranks of senior lecturer, reader, and professor. In essence, the findings show that female academics of senior lecturer rank and above are happier than their male counterparts of comparable rank. In the professorial rank, in particular, the differences between the job satisfaction levels of females and males is considerable (overall job satisfaction score of 5.000 versus 3.946).

Figure 2: Histogram of ANOVA results: rank x gender

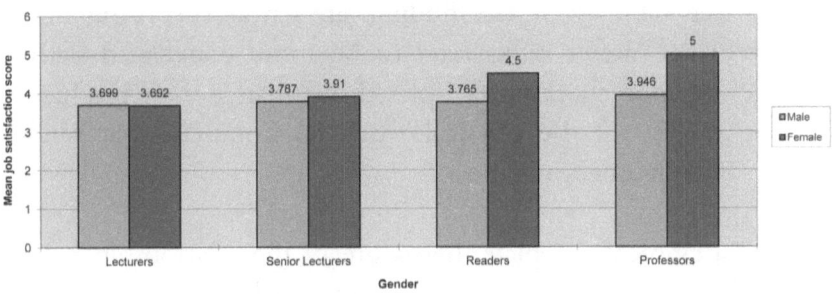

Table 18 also shows ANOVA results for satisfaction with pay, promotion and physical conditions/working facilities that exist in universities. Two results stand out clearly from this table. Satisfaction levels with respect to rank and the interactive effect of rank and gender are significant not only on overall job satisfaction, but also on present pay, promotions, and the physical conditions/working facilities. It is of interest to observe that in respect of satisfaction with promotions, in particular, the variables (rank and the interactive effect of rank and gender), are each significant at a 99 per cent confidence level. The F-values are as high as 12.697 for rank and gender, and 23.699 for satisfaction levels on rank alone! Compared with variables such as age and gender, rank seems to be a significant predictor of job satisfaction in academia.

On present pay and promotion, the interactive effect of rank and age are also statistically significant and the combined interactive effect of rank, gender, and age is significant for physical conditions/working facilities. This means that rank and age together explain job satisfaction on present pay and promotion and job satisfaction on physical conditions/working facilities is explained by the interactive effects of the three variables, gender, rank and age.

Satisfaction derived from physical conditions/working facilities is statistically significant with respect to rank, the interactive effect of rank and gender, and the combined interactive effect of rank, gender and age (see Table 18). These findings are hardly surprising, because employees on higher ranks tend to be more concerned with the adequacy of their working facilities that enhance their productivity, and the quality of the physical work environment that tends to signify status in an organisation.

Figure 3 graphically depicts the nature of the relationship between rank and overall satisfaction, and between rank and satisfaction with present pay, promotion, and physical conditions/working facilities that exist in UK universities. Satisfaction level rises proportionately with rank, lecturers being the least satisfied and professors being the most satisfied. Tests of differences of overall satisfaction levels between the ranks are statistically significant (depicted graphically on Figure 3). Tests of differences for satisfaction levels on present pay, promotions and physical conditions/working facilities are also statistically significant but the nature of the relationships are unique for each consideration (the histograms of Figure 3 depict the nature of each relationship).

Figure 3: Histograms showing the nature of relationships between rank and overall satisfaction and between rank and satisfaction with present pay, promotions, and physical conditions/working facilities which exist in UK universities

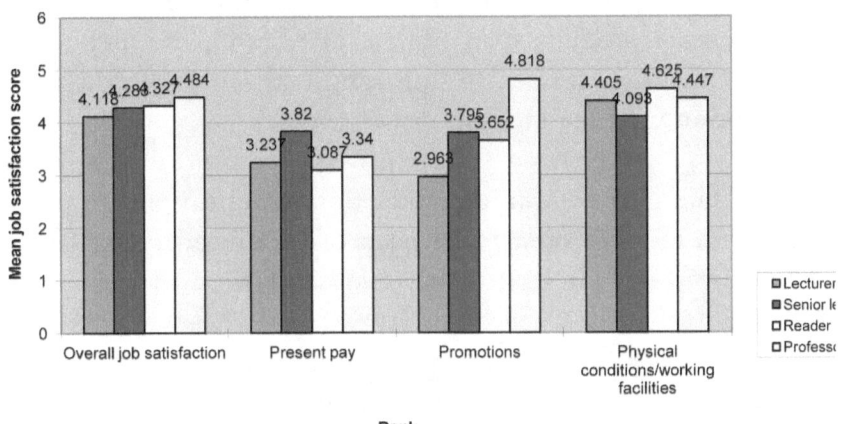

Information on present pay, in Figure 3, shows that satisfaction levels of academics follow the pattern: senior lecturers, professors, lecturers and readers in that order (i.e. senior lecturers are the most satisfied whereas readers are the least satisfied). Results of satisfaction with pay are therefore not dependent on rank although pay levels in universities, as in other organisations, generally reflect rank. One explanation for this possibility is that pay levels at universities overlap from one grade to the next. For example, some senior lecturers, in a post for many years, may receive higher pay than some newly promoted professors. Satisfaction with pay, in the universities, would therefore not seem to be a function of one's rank. Satisfaction with pay may perhaps be more closely related to the size of the family and individual lifestyles.

With promotion, however, professors are naturally the most happy having attained the pinnacle of their academic ladder with all the associated material and non-material benefits. Senior lecturers are ranked second on satisfaction with promotion. Some readers experience frustration with their posts because some are well-qualified professorial candidates with no vacant Chairs to which they can aspire. Lecturers are obviously the least satisfied with promotion because they are at the bottom of the academic ladder. For those who have spent several years in the university system, the impression gained by a lack of promotion is that they may be under-productive in respect of research and publications. Because this is not true in all situations, one can expect some level of frustration with the promotional system.

As the values of the mean job satisfaction scores for present pay and promotions indicate, these two aspects of the university teachers' job are the lowest rated in terms of levels of satisfaction among the eight considerations rated (Oshagbemi, 1996).

Satisfaction with physical conditions/working facilities generally shows higher levels when compared to satisfaction levels on present pay and promotion. Academics of the rank of readers are most happy with this aspect of their job followed by professors, lecturers, and senior lecturers in that order (see Figure 3). Rank does not, therefore, seem to offer any consistent indication of satisfaction level on this aspect of the job. Readers generally have equal access with professors to organisational facilities and in this sense, they may be happier than professors. Similarly, lecturers have comparable facilities to their senior colleagues and in that sense may also be more satisfied compared with senior lecturers. These results show, however, satisfaction with this aspect of a university teachers' job is not consistently related to rank.

Summary and conclusions

This section of the chapter examines the effects of rank on the job satisfaction of UK academics. By analysing the frequency distribution of responses, it was found that overall job satisfaction increases progressively with rank. This finding is supported by a three-way ANOVA that is significant at a 95 per cent confidence level. ANOVA results also reveal that the interaction effect of rank and gender does affect the job satisfaction of university teachers significantly ($p < 0.012$). This means that within certain ranks, gender does affect the job satisfaction of university teachers. Specifically, within the ranks of senior lecturer, reader, and professor, female academics are more satisfied with their jobs when compared to males of comparable ranks. In conclusion, the results of this study generally show that there is a positive association between rank and job satisfaction as has been found in the literature (see, for example, Near et al., 1978).

It should be stated that our results only show the associative relationship between the variables examined. This limitation suggests possible directions for future research. It will be interesting, for example, to investigate how and why rank, among other factors, affects job satisfaction. If rank and certain other effects can be quantified, this will enhance the current literature on job satisfaction.

CHAPTER 9

Length of Service and Job Satisfaction

Introduction

THIS CHAPTER ASKS WHETHER academic workers' length of service is related to their level of job satisfaction. This enquiry is premised on the assumption that less satisfied workers tend to resign whereas workers who are more satisfied tend to remain in a job, as some literature suggests. This research distinguishes between length of service in higher education (LSHE) as a whole, and length of service in present university (LSPU), to separate those academics who have remained within one university from those who have moved from one higher educational institution to another. Two-way analyses of variance confirm the results of the frequency analyses and indicate that, for direct effects and a 0.05 significance level, LSHE is not statistically significant but LSPU is, (p value of 0.022). This means that the overall job satisfaction of university teachers is significantly correlated with LSPU, but not LSHE.

A number of earlier studies suggest that the length of service in a job can be used to estimate the levels of job satisfaction of workers. The assumption is that less satisfied workers tend to resign whereas more satisfied ones tend to remain in a job. Consistent with this thinking a negative relationship between job satisfaction and turnover has been reported by several researchers (Atchinson and Lefferts, 1975; Karp et al., 1973; Locke, 1976; Mobley et al. 1979). This situation should result in a higher average level of satisfaction being reported by employees whose length of service in an organisation is longer, *ceteris paribus*. Other researchers have also reported the same negative relationship between job satisfaction and absenteeism (Porters and Steers, 1973; Scott and Taylor, 1985). These findings suggest that organisations need to better understand factors affecting employee job satisfaction to better manage turnover and absenteeism.

In the university work environment, as indeed in several other organisations, length or duration of service in the same organisation does not necessarily guarantee being promoted to a higher rank. Indeed, some employees change their organisations and engage in job-hopping simply to gain promotion to a higher rank, denied them by their initial organisation. There are several examples of academics who have accepted professorial appointments in other universities when their original universities would not appoint them. For such individuals, the duration of service in the new university may well be short but their rank would be high. Because job satisfaction is an important attribute which organisations desire of their employees, this study asks whether LSPU or in higher education as a whole is related to the level of job satisfaction.

Literature review

Length of service, as used in this study, refers to the number of years an individual has spent working. Research studies designed to investigate whether or not job satisfaction increases with length of service are few. A search of relevant articles through the Institute of Scientific Information Social Sciences Database revealed only seven articles published between 1981 and 1998, inclusive! The search used 'length of service' as keywords in a title during the investigation.

Ronen (1978) examined the relationship between job satisfaction and length of employment in a particular job. He confirmed the hypothesis that the change in job satisfaction with length of service resembles a U-shaped curve. It is suggested that intrinsic satisfaction with a job is a major contributor to changes in the overall satisfaction of workers over time. Thus, according to Ronen, length of service is related to job satisfaction and dissatisfaction. Nicholson and Miljus (1972) concluded in their studies that promotion and salary policies and administrative practices seem to be at the very core of turnover problems. The researchers did not directly relate turnover and length of service to job satisfaction or dissatisfaction.

Abraham and Medoff (1984) presented survey evidence that protection against job loss grows with employees' length of service even after controlling the perceived net value of employees to the firm. Although longer service generally translates into additional protection, we have no evidence that this protection directly increases the job satisfaction level of workers. However, it would be reasonable to expect that protection against arbitrary dismissal directly increases the job satisfaction level of workers, given characteristics of the current job market in the UK. Abraham and Medoff (1985) also provide evidence on the relative importance of length of service and ability in the promotion process. Because promotion is a key variable judged important in the formulation of job satisfaction measures (Imparato, 1972; Smith et al., 1969; Wanous and Lawler, 1972; Scampello and Campbell, 1983), it is logical to link increasing length of service to a greater level of job satisfaction.

In a study of volunteers by Black and DiNitto (1994), satisfaction by both men and women in the work they do was high, because both sexes felt highly accepted in their experience. Indeed, many volunteers reported that they plan to continue volunteering indefinitely. Here, the declared length of service was indefinite, implying that workers want to remain longer in the jobs where they experience a high level of satisfaction. The greater the satisfaction level, the longer workers want to remain in jobs, other aspects being equal. The reverse of this statement is also generally true.

Nevertheless, one must appreciate that in the current employment market in the UK, there will be many workers who will remain in their jobs for economic reasons rather than from satisfaction in these jobs.

Brockner and Kim (1993) investigated factors affecting the job satisfaction of 'stayers' in response to a co-worker who departs for a 'better' job. The study was principally concerned with the consequences of turnover on the job satisfaction of stayers rather than the relationship between length of service and job satisfaction. The three factors that influence the job satisfaction level of stayers did not include length of service. Woodward's (1983) study developed a model for forecasting manpower numbers with classes defined by grade, age and length of service. Although the use of this model was illustrated by projecting age and grade distributions of academics in UK universities, there was no discussion of any link between job satisfaction and length of service.

Although Sagie's work (1998) discusses employee absenteeism, organisational commitment and job satisfaction, it did not explore the relationship between length of service and job satisfaction. It found that 'intention to quit', which is of some relevance to length of service, was not significantly related to either voluntary or involuntary absenteeism. Nathanson and Eggleton's work (1993) with four typologies explored the contrasting motivations and compared the relative importance of these motivations with the importance of a written contract to length of volunteer service. The result of their analyses provides evidence of a relationship between a written contract and length of service. In addition, the frequencies of motivational responses for contract versus non-contract workers, although controlling for length of service, imply an association between these three variables. This finding suggests that endogenous motivation can be as important an influence as an external constraint on length of service.

Gray and Phillips (1994) investigated turnover, age and length of service among nurses and other staff within the UK National Health Service. They found that nurses tend, on average, to have a longer length of service than non-nursing staff groups, whereas it would seem that the average length of service for registered nurses has increased over the past 20 years. However, the authors admit there is a more complex relationship between length of service and turnover and they did not correlate length of service with the level of job satisfaction of the workers.

Siu and Cooper (1998) investigated the direct and moderating effects of locus of control and organisational commitment on the relationship of sources of stress with psychological distress, job satisfaction and the quitting intention of employees working in Hong Kong firms. Results suggest that locus of control and organisational commitment, have strong direct effects and moderating effects on job satisfaction. Although it was thought that organisational commitment was related to length of service, the nature and strength of this possible relationship was not explored.

The relationship between length of service and job satisfaction does not seem to have attracted the attention of many researchers (Oshagbemi, 2000c).

Statistical methods

To study the effect of LSPU and LSHE on the job satisfaction of university teachers, a two-way analysis of variance, (ANOVA), was performed. The direct effects of LSPU and LSHE, and the interactive effects between LSPU and LSHE, were investigated. Investigations included not only overall job satisfaction in relation to LSPU and LSHE, but also satisfaction with present pay, teaching and co-workers in relation to length of service.

Descriptive statistics are computed to examine the overall job satisfaction levels across the different lengths of service of university teachers. In addition, histograms showing the nature of relationships between LSHE and overall satisfaction and between LSPU and overall job satisfaction are presented. Line charts showing relationships between LSHE/LSPU and satisfaction with teaching, co-workers and pay are presented to depict these relationships graphically.

Understandably, respondents who did not change institutions record the same periods for LSPU as in higher education as a whole. For academics who moved from one university to another, and there are many such examples, the number of years recorded in present institution may only be a fraction of the total number of years spent in higher education.

Results and discussion

From Table 19, when LSPU is considered in isolation, the overall job satisfaction score is lowest for workers who have spent ten years or less in their present university (4.148). It increases progressively for each additional ten–year service with a final job satisfaction score of 4.531 for those who have served in excess of 30 years. This suggests that overall job satisfaction increases progressively with length of service in the present university.

Table 19: Breakdown of respondents by length of service in present university/higher education

	Frequency	Percentage	Overall job satisfaction score
Length of service in present university			
1–10 years	273	49.3	4.148
11–20 years	150	27.1	4.203
21–30 years	112	20.2	4.344
31+ years	19	3.4	4.531
Length of service in higher education			
1–10 years	199	35.9	4.195
11–20 years	179	32.3	4.194
21–30 years	143	25.9	4.242
31+ years	33	5.9	4.383

Notes Overall job satisfaction score for all respondents = 4.212; standard deviation = 0.798

Table 19 also shows the overall job satisfaction score for LSHE as a whole, including length of service in the present university. Here, the overall job satisfaction score for workers during the first ten years (4.195) is much the same as for those whose length of service is between 11 and 20 years (4.194). The overall job satisfaction score then increases progressively for academics working from 21 to 30 years (4.242) and for those working beyond 30 years (4.383). It is of interest to note that the overall job satisfaction scores for workers in higher education are, after the first ten years, less than the corresponding job satisfaction scores for those in present universities.

Table 20 presents the ANOVA results that show that, for the direct effects and a 0.5 significance level, (LSHE) is not statistically significant, but (LSPU) is, with a p-value of 0.022. This implies that the job satisfaction of university teachers is significantly dependent on LSPU but not LSHE. The interactive effects between LSHE and LSPU are not statistically significant for overall job satisfaction.

Table 20: ANOVA results: overall[1] job satisfaction and satisfaction with co-workers, teaching and pay

Aspect of job:		Overall job		Teaching		Pay		Co-workers	
Source:	df	Fvalue	Pr > F	Fvalue	Pr > F	Fvalue	Pr > F	Fvalue	Pr > F
LSPU	7	2.372	0.022*	2.377	0.021*	2.514	0.015*	3.674	0.001**
LSHE	7	0.377	0.916	3.607	0.001**	1.193	0.305	2.157	0.037*
LSPU x LSHE	7	1.376	0.216	1.591	0.138	1.206	0.299	2.375	0.022*

Notes: LSPU = Length of service in present universities; LSHE = Length of service in higher education; $*$ = $P < 0.05$; $**$ = $P < 0.01$; Overall[1] job satisfaction was defined as the mean of the summation of the individual job satisfaction measures: satisfaction levels in (teaching + research + administration and management + present pay + promotions + head of unit's supervision + co-workers' behaviour + physical conditions/working facilities)/8.

ANOVA results, showing the nature of relationships between LSHE and overall job satisfaction and between LSPU and overall job satisfaction, are presented graphically in Figure 4. LSPU rises more steeply over the years compared with LSHE, where the rise is not only flatter, but is non-existent during the first two periods, (i.e. during the first 20 years of service). From the histograms in Figure 4, academics with ten or less years of service in higher education are more satisfied with their jobs compared with corresponding academics in present universities. The histograms also show that for the remaining time periods, (i.e. 11-20, 21-30, and 31+ years), academics in present universities experience greater job satisfaction compared with academics in higher education as a whole.

In essence, these findings establish *prima facie* evidence that, after the first ten years, academics not moving from one university to another are more satisfied with their jobs than those who job hop from one university to another. In addition, the job satisfaction of academics who decide to remain in their universities increases not only after the first decade, but also after the second and third decades, (i.e. throughout their career period in the university). The increase in job satisfaction level from decade to decade is statistically significant ($p < 0.05$). Figure 4 gives the mean job satisfaction score in each case.

Figure 4: Histograms showing the nature of relationships between length of service in higher education and overall job satisfaction and between length of service in present university and overall job satisfaction

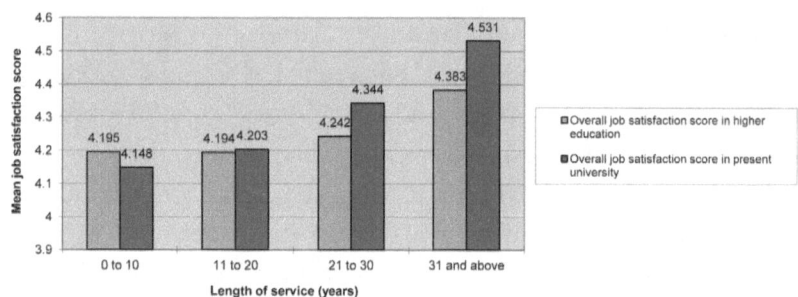

For academics in higher education as a whole, there is a marginal decrease in job satisfaction in the 11-20 year period compared with the job satisfaction level during the first ten years. With the exception of this very marginal decrease (4.195 to 4.194), there is an increase in the job satisfaction of the academics in this category throughout the time period for which data are available. It should be noted, however, that increases in the level of job satisfaction from one period to another are not statistically significant. Compared with academics in higher education, those in present universities generally experience greater job satisfaction levels as evidenced by Table 20 and Figure 4.

Table 20 also shows ANOVA results for satisfaction with pay, teaching and co-workers in universities. Two results stand out clearly from the Table. Satisfaction levels with respect to LSPU are significant not only on overall job satisfaction, but also on teaching, pay and co-workers. The significant levels are 95 per cent each for overall job satisfaction with teaching and pay, and 99 per cent for the satisfaction level with co-workers. Furthermore, satisfaction levels for LSPU, LSHE and LSPU ★ LSHE are each significant in respect of co-workers. This suggests that satisfaction levels with co-workers, either in present university or in higher education as a whole, are high. In addition, for teaching, LSPU and LSHE are each statistically significant whereas the remaining tests in the study are not. ANOVA tests are not significant for other tasks, namely, supervision/supervisor behaviour, administration and management, physical conditions/working facilities, research and promotions in any of the three dimensions (LSPU, LSHE and LSPU ★ LSHE). These dimensions do not therefore explain satisfaction levels of academics with these tasks.

Compared with LSHE as a whole therefore, LSPU seems to be a better indicator/predictor of satisfaction levels of members of academic staff. Although job-hopping may be a factor towards improving promotion for UK academics, it would not seem to substantially increase their overall level of satisfaction with their jobs. Academics who remain within one higher educational institution tend to be more satisfied, on the whole, with their jobs. This may be due to their familiarity with their environment, possibly greater established social contacts, better knowledge of processes and procedures within their organisations, greater family stability and stability within friendship networks.

An implication of this finding is that, although mobility within UK higher education improves the chances of promotion to a higher rank, this incentive does not necessarily lead overall to greater job satisfaction on the part of academics on the move. Job satisfaction is indeed a complex phenomenon involving a multitude of considerations (Cranny et al., 1992). It is of interest to observe from Table 20 that academics who remain in their original universities are more satisfied with their pay *vis-à-vis* those who job-hop and who presumably will be on higher pay as a result. This finding strengthens the opinion that satisfaction with pay may not necessarily be a function of the absolute level of pay but of other considerations about a job and the relative value of pay (Schwab and Wallace, 1974; Lee and Martin, 1996).

Figure 5 gives a series of line charts depicting the nature of relationships between LSHE/LSPU and satisfaction with teaching, co-workers and pay. From the line charts, satisfaction levels are, on the whole, greatest in teaching followed by co-workers and least with pay (Oshagbemi, 1996). In respect of length of service generally, the satisfaction level with teaching is lower in higher education than present universities during the first ten years. After this period, satisfaction levels are consistently lower in present universities compared with higher education. Satisfaction level with co-workers is also lower in higher education compared with present university during the first ten years of working. However, satisfaction with co-workers increases relatively during the second and third decades only to become lower again during the fourth time period.

Figure 5: Line charts showing the nature of relationships between length of service in higher education (HE)/present university (PU) and satisfaction with teaching, co-workers and pay

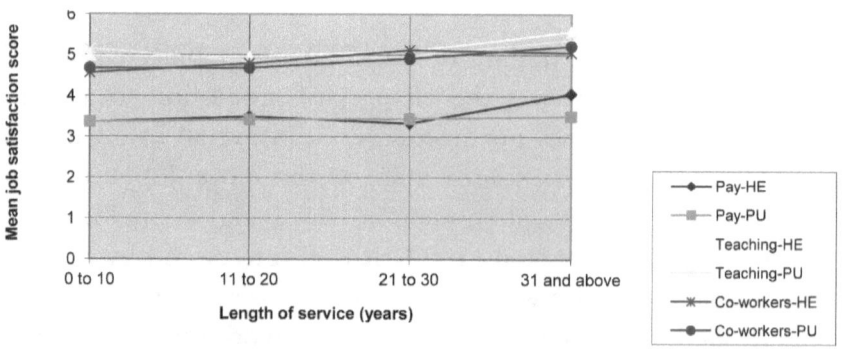

Finally, in respect of length of service, satisfaction level with pay starts lower in higher education, compared to present universities, then higher in the second decade, lower again in the third decade and finally higher in the fourth time period. In the present universities, satisfaction with pay increased consistently from the first time period until the fourth as was the case with satisfaction with co-workers, but not with satisfaction with teaching (see Figure 5). Overall, therefore, academics who job-hop start their careers with higher job satisfaction relative to those who remain in one university during the first ten years. After this period, however, academics who remain in one institution tend to receive greater job satisfaction throughout the rest of their academic careers compared with those who move from one university to another.

Summary and conclusions

Job-hopping in UK universities is a subject of major interest. Some academics may not be offered Chairs in their establishments until another institution offers one in the first instance. In some cases, universities would agree that it is not lack of merit on the part of academics but lack of money to fund higher vacancies if declared. Somehow, however, money is found when an outstanding academic accepts a professorship elsewhere. Some academics move to the institutions that offer them Chairs in the first instance, whereas others remain with their original institutions that equal or better the offer. From this perspective, it seems that job-hopping in UK universities pays towards obtaining professorial rank but not, unfortunately, to increasing the job satisfaction of academics on the move.

This study examines whether length of service is related to level of job satisfaction. It distinguishes between academics who job-hop and those who remain in one higher educational institution. Thus, academics that hop from one university to the other may have a shorter number of years in their present universities but may have several years of service in higher education as a whole. The study attempts to establish whether the job satisfaction of workers who hop from one institution to another tends to be higher or lower compared with those who remain with one employer.

By analysing the frequency distribution of responses to the questionnaire, we found that the overall job satisfaction of academics who stayed in one institution improved significantly with length of service, unlike those who hopped from one institution to another. Furthermore, the levels of overall job satisfaction of those who remained in one institution were, after the first ten years, consistently higher than the corresponding levels of job satisfaction of workers who changed their universities. This finding was supported by a two-way ANOVA, significant at a 95 per cent confidence level. Possible reasons for this result are outlined. ANOVA results also revealed that LSPU is significant, not only to overall job satisfaction, but also to satisfaction in teaching, pay and co-workers.

It would be interesting to investigate how, and why, LSPU, among other factors, affects job satisfaction. It would also be useful if length of service and other effects could be quantified, because this would enhance current literature on job satisfaction.

Chapter 10

Gender and Job Satisfaction

Introduction

This CHAPTER NOTES THAT in recent years there has been a substantial rise in the number of women entering the work-force. One consequence is that this trend has generated considerable interest in the relationship between gender and job satisfaction. An objective of this chapter was to investigate the effects of gender on the job satisfaction of UK academics. The results of the analyses indicate that gender does not directly affect the job satisfaction of university teachers. However, the interactive effect of gender and rank was statistically significant ($p<0.05$). Overall, female academics at higher ranks, namely, senior lecturers, readers and professors, are more satisfied with their jobs than male academics of comparable ranks. The implications of this finding, including other personal correlates of overall job satisfaction are explored.

Statistics in the UK show that women have increasingly become economically active and this trend is projected to continue. For example, in 1971, women made up 37 per cent of the civilian labour force, which rose to 44 per cent in 1993 and is estimated to reach 46 per cent in 2006 (Church, 1995, p.65). The increase in economic activity rates by women is correlated with economic and social changes such as falling birth rates. In universities, however, women account for only about 22 per cent of full time academic staff as of 1993 (Church, 1995, p.66). The percentage of women in academia is thus only half of the percentage of women in overall employment.

An interesting question is whether women academics are, at least, as satisfied with their jobs as their male counterparts. This chapter attempts to answer this question and addresses the effects of gender on the job satisfaction of UK academics. The study also investigates the impact of gender differences on three aspects of the university teachers' job, namely: satisfaction levels with pay, promotions and physical conditions/working facilities. Research studies on gender differences of university teachers are very few indeed, despite the plethora of research on the topic of job satisfaction in general.

Literature review

Several researchers have examined the relationship between job satisfaction and gender (see, for example, Mottaz, 1986; Goh *et al.*, 1991; Mason, 1995). However, the results of the many studies concerning the relationship between job satisfaction and the gender of the employees have been contradictory. Some studies have found women to be more satisfied than men (Bartol and Wortman, 1975; Murray and Atkinson, 1981; Sloane and Williams, 1996; Clark, 1996, 1997; Ward and Sloane, 1998) whereas others have found men to be more satisfied than women (Hulin and Smith, 1964; Weaver, 1974; Shapiro and Stern, 1975; Forgionne and Peeters, 1982). It is important to observe, however, that most of the studies in this area report no significant differences between the sexes in relation to job satisfaction particularly when a number of other variables were statistically controlled (Brief *et al.*, 1977; Golembiewski, 1977; Weaver, 1978; Smith and Plant, 1982; Mottaz, 1986).

A common explanation for the different level of work satisfaction sometimes reported for men and women is that women have different expectations with regard to work (Campbell *et al.*, 1976). Careers are of central importance to men but not as important to women (Kuhlen, 1963). Research has suggested that men and women may use different qualitative criteria in their assessment of work. From this perspective, job satisfaction is seen as an emotional response to the interaction of work rewards and work values. On the one hand the greater the perceived congruence between rewards and values, the greater the job satisfaction—and on the other hand, the greater the perceived discrepancy, the less the satisfaction.

Centres and Bugental (1966) reported other differences. Their research suggested that women placed more value on the social factors of a job than men, and that men valued the opportunity for self-expression in their work more than women. Schuler (1975) found that females in his study valued the opportunities to work with pleasant employees more than males, whereas males regarded the opportunities to influence important decisions and direct the work of others as more important. There is much evidence to support the hypothesis that men and women may differ in terms of work related values (Keith and Glass, 1977; McCarney et al., 1977; Jurgensen, 1978).

Some people see job satisfaction as a function of 'what is expected and what is received'. Thus if one expects little and gets little, one will be satisfied. At the same time, if one expects a lot and gets a lot, one will also be satisfied. However, if one expects a lot but gets little, one will be dissatisfied. The basic argument is that although women receive less from their jobs than men do, they have lower expectations and hence perceive themselves as being just as satisfied as men. A study by Murray and Atkinson (1981) investigated this argument. They reasoned that if the expectancy notion was correct then women should be more satisfied than men if job level and work rewards are held constant. Their findings supported this hypothesis. In this vein, in a study by the Association of University Teachers (Kinman, 1998, p.17), significant gender differences were recorded in perceived job satisfaction. Male respondents, on average, reported that they gained less satisfaction from their jobs compared with females.

The results from a study by Weaver (1977) support the hypothesis that gender and job satisfaction are unrelated, when the effects of other variables are controlled. Findings from a report by Forgionne and Peters (1982) similarly suggest that other factors may be involved in the relationship between gender and job satisfaction, including the number of dependants in a family and the level of management position held in the workplace.

Witt and Nye (1992) evaluated potential gender differences among 12,979 personnel in 30 different organisational systems in

(a) correlates between fairness and job satisfaction scores and
(b) standard group differences in the perceived amounts of pay and promotion fairness and expressed levels of specific and global job satisfaction.

The fairness-satisfaction relationship was not higher for men, and there were no practical differences in fairness perceptions and job satisfaction between men and women. However, Mwamwenda (1997) shows that in a stratified random sample in South Africa, although both male and female teachers expressed a considerable degree of job satisfaction, the general trend was for more male teachers to express job satisfaction than was generally the case with female teachers. This finding lends support to studies carried out in Japan and Germany in which it was shown that more men than women enjoyed teaching as a profession (Lissmann and Gigerich, 1990; Ninomiya and Okato, 1990).

Inconsistencies in findings concerning the relationship between gender and job satisfaction may, therefore, be due to a variety of factors. Not only might males and females in the same organisations differ in job level, promotional prospects, pay and so on, they may differ in the extent to which the same job satisfies their needs. A job high on social satisfaction but low on skill utilisation and career prospects may result in higher job satisfaction for females than for males, whereas in occupations allowing little scope for social relationships, the differences in satisfaction might be in the opposite direction. Given the overall results from these studies, it is apparent that when other variables are taken into account, there is very little evidence to suggest that gender directly influences job satisfaction. There is no compelling reason to believe that given equal education, employment and advancement opportunities, and an equal chance to apply their skills to appropriate challenges, women should be any less satisfied than men with their jobs.

This argument was supported by Ward and Sloane's (1998) study. Their paper considers job satisfaction in the academic labour market drawing upon a particularly detailed data set of 900 academics from five traditional Scottish Universities. Their results show that reports of overall job satisfaction do not vary widely by gender. This result is explained through the nature of their dataset, limited as it is to a highly educated workforce, in which female workers are likely to have job expectations comparable to their male counterparts.

From the 1950's to date, the findings regarding gender differences in job satisfaction have been inconsistent (DeSantis and Durst, 1996). The current investigation examines the effects of gender on the job satisfaction of university teachers, an occupational group yet to be extensively researched although a substantial proportion, if not the bulk, of research activities is undertaken by them (Oshagbemi, 2000e).

Statistical method

To study the effect of gender on the job satisfaction of university teachers, as well as the effects of age and rank, a three-way analysis of variance, (ANOVA), was performed (Edwards, 1979; Bray and Maxwell, 1985; Iversen and Norpoth, 1987). This analysis was used, because the job satisfaction scales used in this study do not violate the assumptions of Gaussian distribution and homogeneity of variance between cells. As indicated in earlier chapters, the questionnaire used eight scales designed to measure satisfaction with respect to different components of university teachers' overall job satisfaction. It will also be recalled that each item in the scale was measured from a range of 1 to 7, 4 representing indifference. Conceptually the indifference zone, 4, represents zero satisfaction. Thus 5, 6, and 7 recorded positive satisfaction, the higher the number, the greater the satisfaction level. Similarly, 1, 2, and 3 recordings represent negative satisfaction, the lower the number, the greater the level of dissatisfaction. The total of the eight scales gives a summary measure of overall job satisfaction.

Results and discussion

From Table 15, female university teachers are marginally more satisfied with their jobs when compared with their male counterparts. The overall job satisfaction score was 4.220 for females versus 4.206 for males. It is also observed from this table that overall job satisfaction scores increase with rank and with age.

These findings are interesting because they suggest that women in academia are marginally more satisfied with their jobs *vis-à-vis* their male counterparts. However, these tentative findings must be confirmed by more rigorous analyses designed to test whether the reported differences between the sexes are statistically significant.

Table 16 presented a further breakdown of the overall job satisfaction scores of the different ranks of university teachers by gender and age group. It is interesting to note that there were no female university readers in the sample and the overall job satisfaction scores of the three female professors were much higher record than the average.

Table 18 shows ANOVA results for overall job satisfaction and satisfaction with pay, promotion and for the physical conditions/working facilities that exist in UK universities. For direct effects on overall job satisfaction, age and gender are not statistically significant but rank is ($p < 0.021$). Hence, there is evidence to show that job satisfaction of university teachers is dependent on rank, after allowing for age and gender. For interactive effects, only the interaction of gender and rank is statistically significant ($p < 0.012$), and although gender by itself is not significantly related to job satisfaction, it is significant when compared together with the rank of university teachers. The ANOVA results of the interactive effects of gender and rank are presented graphically in Figure 2. Please note that only the results for the variables gender and interactions with age and/or rank are discussed, because these are the focus of this section of the chapter.

From the histogram (Figure 2), it will be seen that both male and female lecturers are almost equally satisfied, although female academics experienced higher satisfaction levels than their male counterparts for the ranks of senior lecturer and professor. In essence, the findings show that female academics of senior lecturer rank and above are more satisfied than their male counterparts of comparable ranks. In the professorial rank, the differences between the job satisfaction levels of females and males are considerable (overall mean job satisfaction score of 5.000 versus 3.946). One reason suggested for this result is the relatively few numbers of female workers in top academic ranks. Thus, female readers and professors may see themselves as exceptionally gifted and hardworking in their disciplines, and, this would explain their greater job satisfaction. However, the low number of female professors in this survey denotes caution when making categorical statements that they are more satisfied with their job *vis-à-vis* their male counterparts.

Table 18 also shows ANOVA results for satisfaction with present pay, promotions and physical conditions/working facilities that exist in universities. It is interesting to note that on pay satisfaction, gender, the interactive effect of gender and age, and the interactive effect of gender and rank are all statistically significant ($p < 0.01$). This indicates that the pay satisfaction of university teachers is greatly influenced by gender and the interaction of gender with age or rank. Figure 6 confirms that female satisfaction with pay is higher than that of males (pay satisfaction score of 3.289 for males *versus*

3.599 for females). It is interesting to observe that women are more satisfied with their pay compared with men although their salaries may not be higher. If so, their satisfaction may well be explained by their role in the family, especially if they are not the sole or the primary income earners. Additionally, for female professors, there is the positive psychological dimension to the formal and informal, monetary and non-monetary opportunities that higher rank bestows on incumbents, who, in this case, are few.

Figure 6: Histograms showing the nature of relationships between gender and overall satisfaction and between gender and satisfaction with present pay, promotions and physical conditions/working facilities which exist in UK universities

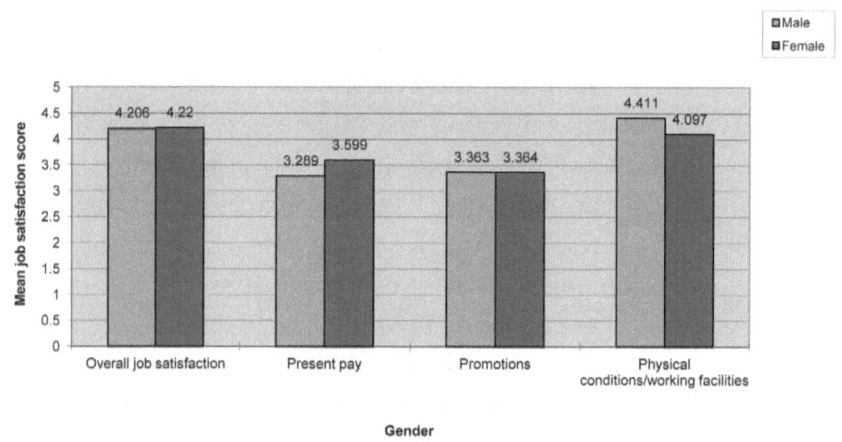

With satisfaction derived from promotions, the interactive effect of gender and rank is statistically significant ($p<0.000$). This means that although gender alone does not explain job satisfaction with promotions, gender and rank together reveal some significant results on this aspect of their job (see Table 18). In particular, women with higher ranks are very satisfied with the promotions in their establishments. Again, this could be because there are only a few in top positions compared with men. It should also be noted, however, that pay and promotion are related in the sense that promotions (higher rank) mean higher pay, other aspects being equal.

Satisfaction derived from physical conditions/working facilities is statistically significant with respect to gender, the interactive effect of gender and rank, and the combined interactive effect of gender, rank and age (see Table 18). These findings are hardly surprising because some women (author's opinion) tend to be more concerned than men with the quality of their physical work environment and the adequacy of their working facilities, and tend to be less satisfied than men with this aspect, as depicted in Figure 6. Here, the overall job satisfaction score of women for physical conditions/working facilities is 4.097 and 4.411 for men. While men tend to be relatively nonchalant, women tend to pay more attention to the adequacy of working facilities and an attractive work environment. This explains the observed significant differences in satisfaction levels of the sexes (author's opinion).

Figure 6 graphically depicts the nature of relationships between gender and overall satisfaction and between gender and satisfaction with present pay, promotions, and the physical conditions/working facilities, that exist in UK universities. From this figure, female academics are only marginally more satisfied with their overall jobs when compared with their male counterparts, and the two sexes are about equally dissatisfied with promotions. There are no significant differences between the sexes on these last two considerations (see Table 18). On pay, however, female academics are more satisfied than males, but less satisfied with the physical conditions/working facilities that exist in their organisations.

Summary, conclusions and implications

This study examines gender differences in the job satisfaction of UK university teachers and found, from the frequency distribution, that female and male academics were more or less equally satisfied with their jobs. The differences between the overall job satisfaction scores of males versus females are not significant when a three-way ANOVA was employed in the analysis. The multivariate statistical analysis showed that, on the effects of gender on job satisfaction, gender by itself does not affect job satisfaction, consistent with the findings of, for example, Gaertner and Ruhe (1983), Senatra (1988) and Larkin (1990). However, within certain ranks, gender does affect the job satisfaction of university teachers. In particular, within the ranks of senior lecturer, reader and professor, female academics were more satisfied with their jobs than males of comparable ranks.

In conclusion, it must be stated that results show the associative relationship between gender and job satisfaction but do not suggest a cause–effect relationship. This limitation suggests possible directions for future research. It would be interesting to investigate how and why gender, among other factors, affects job satisfaction. It will be useful if gender and other effects could be quantified, because this would enhance current literature on job satisfaction. It is hoped that this study will contribute towards the literature on job satisfaction of university teachers. There seem to be no direct effects of gender on such satisfaction. Effects present are a factor of an employee's rank.

CHAPTER 11

Related studies, summary and conclusions

Introduction

THERE ARE A VARIETY of job satisfaction studies which may not directly be under the current title but which add to our overall knowledge of the subject. These related groups of studies will be reviewed below. The intention is to demonstrate the multidimensional nature of the construct and show the various ways researchers have examined it or aspects of it. It also shows that job satisfaction studies are truly global, and whether positively or negatively, job satisfaction affects all workers. We would review the literature in the following six areas, which are not exhaustive, but reflect areas where the author has had first-hand experiences.

1. satisfaction with line managers' supervision,
2. satisfaction with co-workers' behaviour,
3. pay satisfaction,
4. satisfaction with promotion,
5. satisfaction with the primary tasks and
6. is the time spent on a task related to the level of its enjoyment?

Literature review on the satisfaction derived from line managers' supervision

It is logical to expect that academics will tend to be more satisfied with the behaviour/supervision of their line managers if the universities systematically organise management development programmes for managers. Bone and Bourner (1998) investigated the extent to which such practices occurred in UK universities. According to responses to their postal survey, about half of UK universities provide some organised management development for their managers with the other half doing little to develop their managers in any systematic way. It was suggested that, on this basis, universities provide less management development for their managers than most other UK organisations.

Lacy and Sheehan (1997) examined aspects of academics' satisfaction with their job across eight nations, namely, Australia, Germany, Hong Kong, Israel, Mexico, Sweden, the U K and the USA. The authors examined the impact of context elements, including working climate and atmosphere, on general levels of job satisfaction. The results of their study indicate that relationships with their colleagues, among other factors, are the greatest predictors of job satisfaction. The implications for university management and governing bodies are self-evident. If academic staffs are to be encouraged to express higher levels of job satisfaction or lower levels of job dissatisfaction, attention must be paid to the environment ('climate' or 'atmosphere') in which they work. This includes the behaviour of, and supervision by their line managers.

An article by Lewis (1992) compares, the handling of subordinates, interactions with supervisors, and job satisfaction of men and women in middle-management positions in a federal civil service. Management of problem employees does not differ significantly between sexes, but women have more problems with their supervisors than do men. Overall, women are as satisfied as men with the fairness of their treatment, but the women are much more likely to say they have recently lost a job or job reward due to discrimination against their gender. A study of Indian managers (Viswesvaran et al., 1998), the researchers found that perceived top management support for ethical behaviours was highest with supervision among all five facets of job satisfaction (supervision, pay, promotion, work and co-workers). In such an organisational context workers are relatively most satisfied with the behaviour/supervision of their line managers and these findings have implications for managing either a global workforce or a particular workforce. Cultural differences might have contributed to the findings reported here, and such findings may not be replicated, say in the USA, where managers may not accept the decisions of top managers as passively as the Indians.

In one study, which investigated the interactive effect of information asymmetry and decentralisation on the job satisfaction level of unit managers (Chia, 1995), the results indicate that a higher level for information asymmetry was associated with a higher level of job satisfaction for managers working under conditions of high decentralisation. As the study focused only on managers, there is no comparable information for non-managerial workers. The study by Lam (1997) examines job satisfaction of quality managers and found that their major job 'satisfiers' were pay and promotion. Job recognition and a good relationship with other employees were also perceived to be important in improving job satisfaction among quality managers. Again, a comparison between the managers and the workers' levels of job satisfaction was not made. There was also no direct study of how satisfied the workers were with the behaviour/supervision of their line managers.

An article by Mayfield et al., (1998), bridges theory and practice to show that supervisors' use of 'motivating language theory' correlates significantly with subordinates' performance and job satisfaction. In brief, the theory predicts that strategic applications of leader oral communication have positive measurable effects on subordinate performance and job satisfaction. This theory was tested by the authors using a LISREL analysis and found to be true. A study by Clayton et al. (1998) assessed the impact that work-related factors have on home and family life for female managers in health care food service. The 'number of hours worked' was the employee attribute found to play a statistically significant role in predicting the overall effect of job on home life. Only female managers were studied. There was no comparison of job satisfaction and family life with non-managerial employees.

A study by Marchese and Delprino (1998) asked whether supervisors and subordinates see eye-to-eye on job enrichment. The study compared supervisors' and their subordinates' perceptions of the subordinates' job enrichment. The convergence of these perceptions was then examined in relation to the subordinates' job satisfaction, performance and organisational commitment. The results indicate that: (1) supervisors and their subordinates perceive subordinates' job characteristics differently, and (2) supervisors' perceptions have limited relationships to critical work outcomes.

Evans (1997) highlighted the importance of factors such as leadership and professional orientation, relative perspective and realistic expectation as morale and job satisfaction determinants in his own research, which was carried out in England.

In an article by Trowler (1997), the author argues that there is an urgent need to emphasise the role of the academic as an important actor in the study of policy implementation in higher education. The study highlighted ways in which academics respond to changing contexts and take actions, which have the effect, intentionally or otherwise, of changing policy outcomes. Forgionne and Peeters' (1982) study examines the influence of gender on satisfaction with job-related factors, overall job motivation and overall job satisfaction among managers. The findings suggest that male managers, more than female managers, in first-level positions, indicate a greater overall job satisfaction. Female managers with little formal education are found to be less motivated overall than male colleagues.

Findings by Bone and Bourner (1998) discussed earlier are consistent with those of Mackay (1995a, 1995b) which are based on research in universities in the north of England. Mackay concludes in his articles that in labour intensive organisations, such as universities, the failure to empower the personnel function is somewhat short-sighted given the growing number of government policies directed towards the activities of academic staff. Mackay's research did not, however, deal directly with the satisfaction of academics with the behaviour of their line managers. However, it can be inferred from his articles that in UK universities, academics' satisfaction levels with the supervision of their line managers can be improved.

The work by Winstead et al. (1995) suggests that it is the quality of friendships in the workplace, rather than the formal role of managers and workers, that determines the level of job satisfaction of all concerned. Their findings indicate that, generally, individuals who perceive that they have better interpersonal friendships with their co-workers and immediate supervisor report higher job satisfaction. Their results are consistent with those of Robinson et al. (1993) and Everly and Falcione (1976). Indeed work by Hui and Yee (1999) found a positive correlation between collectivism and job satisfaction but only among members of congenial workgroups. This shows that if academics and their line managers' work together as congenial workgroups, academics will tend to be more satisfied with the behaviour of their line managers.

How satisfied academics were with the behaviour/supervision of their line managers was investigated by Oshagbemi (2001c). His study found that about half of the respondents expressly stated they are satisfied with the behaviour/supervision of their line managers. The remaining 50 per cent of the respondents were either indifferent or downright dissatisfied. The results of multiple regression analyses showed that age and length of service in higher education are important variables that throw some light on the satisfaction/dissatisfaction of academics with the behaviour of their line managers. In particular older academics, tend to be more satisfied with their line managers, however, the longer academics have worked in higher education, the less the satisfaction derived from the behaviour of line managers.

Literature review on the satisfaction derived from co-workers' behaviour

Weaver (1998) reports that evidence from nation-wide opinion surveys from 1972 through to 1996 provides strong evidence that in the US labour force African-Americans reported being less satisfied than Euro-Americans with their jobs. This difference existed for both women and men across categories of education, age and occupation. However, the study did not specifically test satisfaction with co-workers' behaviour. A study by Ganzach (1998) examines the relationship between intelligence and job satisfaction and found that intelligence has a direct negative effect on job satisfaction. The study did not concern itself with the impact of intelligence on satisfaction with co-workers' behaviour.

In a study by Evans (1997), the effects on individual teachers of prevailing context-specific circumstances and of specific events are described, highlighting the importance, as morale and job satisfaction determinants, of factors such as leadership and individuals' professional orientations, relative perspectives and realistic expectations. It is presumed that co-workers' behaviour is significant in such a context although it is not specifically referred to in the study.

Spinelli and Gray (1998) looked at employee job satisfaction within different departments of a major hotel chain. The results not only reflect the importance of non-economic job enrichment factors to job satisfaction but also show that the factors determined to be most important may vary among departments and presumably, among co-workers. Thus, as expected, co-workers' behaviour would be a significant component of overall satisfaction in the hotel industry. Recognition of such variances may help departmental managers more precisely target job enrichment initiatives to their employees' and co-workers' needs.

A remarkable and authoritative study (Schofield, 1998) shows decisively that the manner in which people are managed has a powerful impact on both productivity and profitability. Levels of job satisfaction and organisational commitment were measured among employees in 67 firms. It was found that five per cent of the variation between companies in their profitability, and 16 per cent in their productivity, could be explained by variations in the job satisfaction of their employees. Satisfaction with co-workers' behaviour is an important component of overall job satisfaction.

The behaviour of fellow academics in the same institution was researched by Oshagbemi (2000b) who found out that about 70 per cent of the respondents were satisfied, very satisfied or extremely satisfied with their co-workers' behaviour. The results of a three-way analysis of variance showed that female academics are as satisfied with their co-workers' behaviour when compared to their male colleagues. When rank was examined in relation to co-workers' satisfaction, however, readers were most satisfied, followed by professors, senior lecturers and lecturers in that order. The differences in satisfaction levels with rank and co-workers' behaviour are statistically significant at a 90 per cent confidence level. When examined, age was statistically significant at a 95 per cent confidence level in relation to this consideration. This means that age explains the level of satisfaction with co-workers' behaviour—older workers deriving more satisfaction compared to younger ones.

Literature review on pay satisfaction

Various behavioural scientists have put forth conflicting positions over the meaning of pay satisfaction. On the one hand, researchers such as Herzberg (1966, pp. 71-90) classified pay as a 'hygiene factor' in the work environment and maintained that pay can only lead to feelings of dissatisfaction, but not to satisfaction. On the other hand, discrepancy theorists such as Locke (1969) and Porter (1961) posit that satisfaction is a function of employee's comparison of what exists in their job with what they seek in the job. Pay satisfaction happens when existing pay corresponds to, or is greater than, desired pay, whereas pay dissatisfaction occurs when existing pay is less than desired pay. Equity theories proposed by Jacques (1961), Patchen (1961) and Adams (1965) similarly view pay satisfaction as a continuum possessing both positive and negative values.

Most research efforts, focusing on the correlates of pay satisfaction, have centred on individual and organisational variables. Schwab and Wallace (1974) and Lawler (1971) reviewed a substantial amount of the relevant literature. Unfortunately, most of the studies reviewed by Lawler suffer from a major criticism in that they are mainly uni-variate studies, considering pay satisfaction or another variable. Lawler points out that, as a consequence, it is often '. . . impossible to tell whether the relationship found between a variable and pay satisfaction is due to the effect of the variable studied or another variable' (Lawler, 1971, p. 221). For example, while some researchers report that pay satisfaction is positively related to organisational level (Andrews and Henry, 1963; Rosen and Weaver, 1960), others report that when pay level is controlled, the evidence suggests that pay satisfaction is negatively related to organisational level (Lawler and Porter, 1963).

According to Taylor and Vest (1992), when deciding if they are fairly paid, people look at both the absolute and the relative amount of pay. The results of their studies suggest that external comparisons, such as workers in other organisations or with other employers, may lower pay satisfaction whereas personal comparisons, such as relatives or household members, tend to increase pay satisfaction. The authors explain that the major reason why scholars have investigated the issue of pay satisfaction for decades is the behavioural outcomes believed to accompany pay dissatisfaction. For example, research findings suggest that compensation policies and amounts: influence level of absenteeism (Mobley et al., 1979), influence turnover decisions (Finn and Lee, 1972), and workers' decisions on their productivity (Mahoney, 1979). Hence, pay satisfaction is not only an issue of financial adequacy, but also of psychological adequacy.

Indeed, it is important to recognise that pay is a psychological as much as an economic phenomenon. A study by Lee and Martin (1996) found that the employees' loss of high-tier status possibly explained pay dissatisfaction when they changed from high-tier to low-tier jobs. This is despite the fact that their pay was increased in the low-tier jobs. Klein and Maher (1966) in their sample found that higher education is associated with relative dissatisfaction with pay. In a study by Oshagbemi (1997b), overall job satisfaction was positively and significantly related to rank but not to gender or age. Professors were most satisfied with their overall jobs followed by readers, senior lecturers and lecturers in that order.

Kovach (1993) surveyed over 900 employees in manufacturing jobs across a number of industrial organisations in the USA to determine levels of pay and benefits and satisfaction level with each of these. He found, among other aspects, that, in the area of pay, workers in private organisations received higher absolute levels, and were more satisfied with their monetary compensation than workers in public organisations. In the area of benefits, however, the relationship reverses with public sector employees receiving better benefits and indicating a higher level of satisfaction.

Employee satisfaction with their pay was also a subject of investigation by Oshagbemi (2000a). Unfortunately, despite numerous studies of pay comparisons and pay satisfaction among public and private sector workers, little is known about correlates of employee satisfaction with pay. The author investigated the correlates of pay satisfaction amongst UK academics. The study found that over 50 per cent of the respondents expressly stated that they were dissatisfied with their pay. The results of a three-way analysis of variance showed that female academics are more satisfied with their pay in comparison to their male colleagues. When rank was examined in relation to pay, senior lecturers were most satisfied, followed by professors, lecturers and readers in that order. The differences in satisfaction levels by rank and gender are statistically significant. However, there are no statistical differences in age variations relating to satisfaction with pay.

Roberts and Chonko (1994) investigated the relationship of satisfaction with pay and turnover (the intention to seek new jobs) for men and women in sales. The study found no difference in the effect satisfaction with pay had on men and women's intention to seek new jobs. Vest et al., (1994) investigated the relationship of self-rated performance to pay level satisfaction. Self-rated performance exhibited a significant negative relationship with pay satisfaction.

One possible explanation why men are significantly more dissatisfied than women with their pay is that in some families, it is only the men who work full time while women stay at home, at least for part of the time, to give birth to and rear their children. From this perspective, pay and career may be less important to women. It is little wonder, therefore, that the rank of females is significantly lower than the rank of males in UK universities (Oshagbemi, 1997b). For example, in a publication (*Times Higher Education Supplement,* 1998a), it was revealed that just 7 per cent of professors in the UK are women. This compares with 14 per cent in Australia and 18 per cent in the USA. Indeed, only 3 per cent of UK science professors are women according to this source. These comments partly explain the background between gender and satisfaction with pay. According to a publication by the Association of University Teachers (AUT), many women complained about the negative impact of work on their family lives and expressed difficulty in maintaining an appropriate balance between demands of work and the home (Kinman, 1998, p.17).

Women themselves suggested some form of systematic discrimination against them (Davidson and Burke, 1994). For example, Goffee and Nicholson (1994, p.81) suggested that although females are more highly educated than men they are much less likely to occupy senior managerial positions in organisations. The authors further suggested that where women do work in jobs that are comparable to male colleagues, they tend to be paid less.

In a major study comparing salaries, with the USA as a benchmark, (*Times Higher Education Supplement*, 1998b) researchers calculated that the real salaries of UK academics are as much as 36 per cent lower. Of the eight countries considered in the study, namely, the USA, Australia, the UK, Canada, Hong Kong, New Zealand, Singapore and South Africa, only South African academics are paid less than UK academics. However, the researchers noted that some academics may choose to trade material reward for superior quality of life and that using the 'places to live' of the *Economist,* Australia is the best place to live overall, because it has the best quality of life and the highest real academic salaries of the developed nations. Using this consideration, despite 'very low' academic salaries, the quality of life makes the UK 'quite attractive', according to the authors.

In a recent call to get tough on gender bias, it was suggested at an AUT women's annual meeting that women formed nearly half of the higher education workforce yet were concentrated in the lowest grades and had the worst pay. The General Secretary of the AUT reportedly stated that an average female academic in a UK university will earn between four and five years less salary than an equivalent man working the same number of years between starting and retiring (*Times Higher Education Supplement*, 1999a). It was also suggested by the same source that men's salary, as a percentage of women's could be as high as 114 per cent in the university system.

The 'Athena Project', launched by the Science Minister, Lord Sainsbury, was poised to raise the profile of women in UK universities (*Times Higher Education Supplement,* 1999b). This project focussed mainly on women in science, engineering and technology, and was set up for institutional audits, and support research on barriers to women's progress, confidence building and flexible working. The project aimed to achieve a 10 per cent rise in the number of women in academic posts at all levels five years after the set up date. The project now needs a review to ascertain the extent to which it has accomplished its objectives.

Literature review on employee satisfaction with promotion

Konrad and Cannings (1997) argue that the managerial advancement process is different for women and men. The authors claim that women in management experience statistical discrimination, meaning that they are viewed with suspicion and their commitment and competence is over-tested. Findings from data collected in two large firms supported the gender role congruence and statistical discrimination perspectives. One can therefore infer that women, in their sample, are less satisfied with their promotions compared with men. Powell and Butterfield (1997) investigated whether applicant race and gender interact to influence promotion decisions for top management positions. They found that applicant race indirectly affected promotion decisions through job relevant variables to the disadvantage of applicants of colour. However, women of colour did not experience the negative effects of race that were experienced by men who were non-white.

Sheridan et al., (1997) examined the effects that a manager's formal education, on-the-job training, race and gender had on the probability of being promoted from different jobs during his or her career in a company. They found, among other aspects, that there was no evidence of gender or race discrimination effects. Joy (1998) tested the hypothesis that women face discrimination in promotions in school administration using data from the National Centre for Education Statistics. Results show that men are more likely than women to be selected for promotion during a school year.

Ariga et al., (1997) emphasise talent in the promotion process rather than any socio-demographic variables such as age, gender or rank.

Their model predicts that more talented workers are promoted earlier and they experience not only higher wages but also higher wage growth. Toren (1993) discussed gender inequality in academic careers and argued that because research productivity is the principal basis for promotion in academia, women progress more slowly, hold lower ranks, and are older at each rank than comparable men. This is because they are judged not to be as productive in research publications when compared with their men.

A study by Snell and Baldwin (1987) investigated the extent to which managers, MBA students and professors have similar perspectives regarding the importance of factors in attaining promotions. The study found that managers and professors did not significantly differ in their views. However, MBA students differed from managers and professors in the level of importance they attached to several promotion factors. Swimmer (1990), set out to determine whether there were differences in the promotional chances of male and female clerical employees. The results clearly demonstrated that there was a *prima facie* case of discrimination against women with regards to promotion to junior levels of management compared with their male counterparts.

Hersch and Viscusi (1996), using an original data set in their study, indicate that women receive more promotions than men whereas Lewis (1986) found strikingly similar promotion probabilities for White men and women, once a variety of individual characteristics are accounted for. In Killingsworth and Reimers' (1983) study, the authors found racial and gender differentials in promotions that worked to the disadvantage of non-Whites and women respectively.

According to a study by Eberts and Stone (1985), however, significant apparent gender discrimination in promotions that were present in the early 1970's, had declined by more than half by the late 1970's. Abraham and Medoff (1985), provide evidence on the relative importance of length of service and ability in the promotion process, and that the weight assigned to length of service is significantly greater in union than in non-union settings. Paulin and Mellor's (1996) article empirically tested and confirmed the proposition that the gender-race composition of an employee's occupation significantly affects the likelihood of promotion. They found that White females and minorities were adversely affected in promotions compared to White males and non-Blacks. Fairburn and Malcomson (1994) question why several employers often promote workers to a different job rather than pay workers more for performing their current jobs well. The answer they found lies in the psychological rewards associated with promotion which salary increases alone would not satisfy.

Oshagbemi (2001b) investigated one aspect of manpower development for workers—promotion. Specifically, the satisfaction of academics with their promotions is researched, and the relationships of promotion satisfaction with age, gender and rank are explored. The study found that over 50 per cent of the respondents expressly stated that they were dissatisfied with their promotions. The result of a three-way analysis of variance revealed that male academics are as dissatisfied with their promotion as their female counterparts. In addition, there were no significant differences in age with respondents' satisfaction with their promotions because most of them are approximately equally dissatisfied. However, among the various seniority levels, statistically significant differences exist in the satisfaction levels enjoyed with promotions.

According to a publication by the Association of University Teachers, the pressure to publish emerged as a more potent cause of dissatisfaction for women (Kinman, 1998, p.17). Women also complained about the negative impact of work on family lives and expressed difficulty in maintaining an appropriate balance between demands of work and the home. It can be understood from this background why women do not publish as much as men and consequently why their ranks are not generally as high as the ranks of male colleagues.

The *Times Higher Education Supplement* (1999b) annual league table of women professors showed less than one in ten professors was female. Women in the UK, who make up a third of academic staff, are not alone in having a hard time breaking into the top ranks. The USA is better, but there too the imbalance is stark. Only 20 per cent of full-time professors are women, and their salary averages 79 per cent that of men's. This means that discrimination is not confined to promotion because there is a pay gap for women as well. This is contingent on the fact that minimum professorial salary is set around £55,000 per annum. One pointer to the problem is that few of the women who make it to professor rank have children. As with high-flyers in many professions, the crucial breaks tend to come when people are in the thirties. Promotion depends heavily on publications. Anyone who has taken time out in these years—many of them are women—risk being at a disadvantage. Consequently only 9.2 per cent of UK professors were women in 1998 compared to 6.7 per cent in 1995 (*Times Higher Education Supplement,* 1999d). The percentage of women in all academic grades in 1998 was 33.8 per cent compared to 32.9 per cent in 1997. There is thus a slight increase in the percentage of female academics and professors.

This increase was sustained in 2000 when it was reported that 9.8 per cent of professorships were held by women (*Times Higher Education Supplement,* 2000, pp.18-19). The same source, which ranks universities by their proportion of female professors, revealed striking differences among institutions. At the University of East London, women hold 37.5 per cent of professorships, and at South Bank University, women hold 30.9 per cent, but Bradford University had only 3.4 per cent female professors and the University of Salford only 2.1 per cent. During the 1997-1998 academic year, the proportion of female professors was highest in education (20.1 per cent) and languages (15.9 per cent) and lowest in engineering and technology (2.1 per cent). During the 1998-1999 academic year, the proportion of female professors was still highest in education (21.5 per cent) and languages (17.0 per cent) and still lowest in engineering and technology (2.7 per cent). However, it is clear that the percentage of female professors in UK universities is increasing.

In a *Times Higher Education Supplement* (1999c), it was reported that Cambridge University is expected to award long-awaited promotions to more than 200 academics following the historic concession that staff promotions will in future be based on merit—not on budget constraints. In 1996, the University admitted that it did not have the resources to promote all deserving staff. Advocates for promotion on merit argue that personal promotions should be primarily determined by assessments of academic merit without budgetary restraint. This U-turn is expected to reflect practice already in place at Oxford University, where titular promotions can be made without salary enhancements. Campaigners believe that hundreds of deserving academics will have to be given readerships or professorships, after years of being victims of funding constraints. However, some people find it odd that some academics could be 'promoted' as readers, yet left on a senior lecturer's pay!

Literature review on workers' satisfaction with their primary tasks

The primary tasks of academics fall into three areas, namely, teaching, research and administration and management. Together these tasks constitute the basic work of academics, although it can be argued that administration and management is of lesser importance to academics when compared to the other two tasks. Indeed some argue that the primary concern of academics is research excellence and that both the other two tasks are of secondary importance. These different viewpoints represent principal contentions in a debate of what is required from universities (Oshagbemi, 1988, pp.148-153). What is not contestable is that the work of academics is an important organisational activity, which may affect the job satisfaction or dissatisfaction of the workers.

This section of the chapter examines how satisfied academics are with their primary tasks of teaching, research and administration and management and undertakes an assessment of the relative satisfaction levels among the three tasks, which are core aspects of their job. Table 21 details the percentage distribution of the time spent by academic managers on their primary tasks. It shows that administration and management accounts for more than 50 per cent of the time spent by academic managers whereas teaching and research activities only account for less than 50 per cent of their time.

Furthermore the section considers whether satisfaction levels in each of these three tasks is related to the age, rank or gender of the academics. Rather than adding these three tasks together and treating the sum of the tasks as constituting the work of academics, it was decided to examine each task independently. There are often significant differences in the satisfaction levels received by various individuals in the performance of each of the three tasks or sets of activities.

A review of the few relevant research studies undertaken will include those of Gruneberg *et al.,* 1974a, 1974b; Startup *et al.,* 1975; Gruneberg and Startup, 1978; Startup and Gruneberg, 1973, 1976; and those of Nicholson and Miljus, 1972. One of these studies discussed the relationship of turnover decisions by sampled university teachers with overall job satisfaction. Other studies were concerned with the university teachers' satisfaction with one or two facets of their job such as teaching, research, or promotional prospects. None of the studies was directly concerned with satisfaction with the job of administration and management.

This section is an examination of the core responsibilities of academics. It reflects on sustainable development in higher education and probes how satisfied academics are with their primary tasks of teaching, research and administration and management (Oshagbemi, 2000d). The study found that some 65 per cent of the university teachers were satisfied, very satisfied or extremely satisfied with research. Figures for teaching and administration and management are about 80 and 40 per cent respectively. This study investigated operational aspects of universities and in particular, whether satisfaction with each of their core tasks was related to age, gender or rank. Results show that significant associations exist between age and satisfaction in the core aspects of the university teachers' job. However the nature of the impact of age on the job satisfaction of academics varies from one aspect of the job to another. The nature of the relationships between age and research, teaching and administration and management is not clear, although the relationships themselves are statistically significant. Although it seems that, generally, the older one is the greater the satisfaction enjoyed by teaching and administration and management, the reverse seems true in respect of research satisfaction. The results also reveal, expectedly, that research satisfaction was related to rank—the higher the rank, the greater the level of research satisfaction. It was also found that satisfaction by gender is not related to teaching, research or administration and management.

Table 21: The percentage distribution of the time spent by academic managers on their primary tasks

Task	Percentage time spent by academic managers
Teaching	25.3
Research	24.0
Administration and	50.7
management	100.0

Source: Adapted from Oshagbemi, T (1999), *Managers and their Time*, Blackhall Publishing, Dublin, pp. 49-50.

Is the time spent on a task related to the level of its enjoyment?

One would expect the time spent on a task to be related to the level of its enjoyment because human beings tend to spend more time on what they enjoy doing most. To find out whether this was or was not the case academic managers' allocation of their time amongst their primary tasks of teaching, research and administration and management was investigated. 'Academic managers' are defined here as academics occupying administrative positions such as heads of departments, deans, directors and vice-chancellors. Important to our definition is the requirement that the academic manager must occupy a formal administrative position within the university organisational complex. He or she must also be directly in charge of some colleagues who are invariably both academic and administrative staff (Oshagbemi, 2001a).

The question posed is whether academic managers derive satisfaction from performing their major tasks commensurate with the time spent on these tasks. Using a published work (Oshagbemi, 1999), the issues are examined and it is found that, whereas academic managers spend a smaller percentage of time on teaching and research, relative to the satisfaction derived from performing these tasks, they spend a higher percentage of their time on administration and management. Although there are several studies reporting industrial and other organisational managers' use of their time (see for example, Hanika, 1963; Horne and Lupton, 1965; Dahl and Lewis, 1975; Hinrichs, 1976; Stewart, 1988; Martinko and Gardner, 1990), very few studies document academic managers' allocation of their time.

From Figure 7, it is clear that academic managers derive more satisfaction from teaching (44.2 per cent) compared to time spent on this task (25.3 per cent). Without doubt, teaching is one of the core activities of university teachers. To demonstrate its importance, UK universities now have teaching assessment following the introduction of the research assessment exercise. University teachers are now introduced to training in teaching skills, student assessment and many universities implement peer review of teaching. There are specific training programmes in small group teaching, preparing and giving lectures and teaching larger classes. Knowledge of a subject is one of the criteria used for appointing academics, and this is manifested in the love that many academics have for the dissemination of knowledge in their subject areas.

Figure 7: Histograms showing satisfaction derived from the primary tasks of academic managers compared with the time spent on these tasks

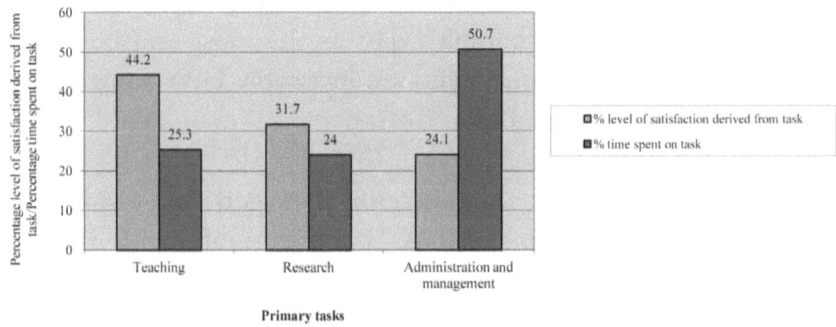

With research, a similar pattern of findings to that for teaching exists: a greater percentage of people (31.7) are satisfied with the task compared with time spent on this task (24.0). However the percentage difference between the time spent versus the satisfaction derived from research is less than that found with teaching (see Figure 7). The ratio of percentage satisfaction obtained *versus* time spent on teaching is 1.747 compared with 1.321 for research. This result is somewhat surprising as the importance of research in universities is well known, and it is the primary criterion used to promote academics to higher ranks, especially at the readership and professorship levels. Indeed some people argue that research excellence is the essence of universities and that the university cannot be an excellent teaching institution if it is devoid of research (Flexner, 1930, p.24; Truscot, 1943, p.45; Audu, 1972, p.61).

Figure 7 depicts a graphical relationship between academic managers' satisfaction with administration and management (24.1 per cent) versus the time spent on the task (50.7 per cent). Unlike teaching and research, where academic managers derive more satisfaction compared to time spent on the tasks, academic managers derive less satisfaction with administration and management *versus* the time spent on this task. The ratio of percentage satisfaction derived *versus* the time spent on administration and management is 0.475. Academic managers therefore spend a lot of time with administration and management and the information from the figures suggests that they are not particularly satisfied with performing this task.

Without doubt, the execution of administration and management activities in universities, as in any other organisation, requires a lot of time. It is almost impossible to be active in teaching and research and in administration and management all at the same period of time. Yet, this is what most academics have to juggle. Although routine administrative tasks can be performed rather quickly (or can be delegated to administrative staff members), some ceremonial events and strategic duties require the undivided attention of academic managers. Success in administration and management was not well rewarded until certain universities expressly used success in this task to promote holders to senior lecturers. It is suggested by some academics that in the future success in administration and management or teaching could be a criterion used for promoting some academics to professorship. However, such a step would downgrade research excellence and would make holders of promotions to professorships, other than by research excellence, hardly worth their titles.

In the past, and currently in some universities in the UK, academic leadership was invariably 'imposed' on professors of whom some saw it as a 'cost' of holding Chairs. For those who voluntarily apply to become academic managers, however, and some people in this group are not professors, a question to be asked is whether they are relatively more competent at performing administration and management activities compared to teaching or research? If so, why do they generally tend to have lower satisfaction levels performing this task compared to the satisfaction level from teaching and research? The benefits associated with performing administrative tasks should also be explored, (such as promotion to senior lecturer and reader and recognition/prominence in organisational activities, such as selection and promotion processes) *vis-à-vis* the attendant costs which include spending a lot of time on university administration. Answers to such questions would need to be investigated before one can be sure of the motivations and incentives of voluntary academic managers.

Summary and conclusions

One should perhaps begin by observing that an argument often brought against theories of job satisfaction is that they take little account of differences between people. The needs of one group of individuals from a job, is often different from the needs of another group. Personal correlates of job satisfaction have become a recent focus of some researchers' interest. Investigators have examined such individual correlates of job satisfaction as physical, mental and dispositional differences. Chapters 7, 8 and 10 reviewed the research that examines how differences between individuals affect job satisfaction, and specifically the influence of age, gender and rank. A main objective of the discussion is to ascertain whether age, rank and gender are personal correlates of overall job satisfaction, within the higher education sector. Clarifying the impact of these demographic variables on the satisfaction of UK academics, may help towards a better understanding of the reasons for different levels of job satisfaction among various categories of academics. Additionally, this information will be of value in the management of universities, a very topical subject in the UK. Consequently, this section summarises conclusions and implications for further studies.

From the literature review, whilst research on individual differences is of considerable importance, a lot of work still needs to be done. Evidence suggests that some organisational factors are more important than individual differences alone. It has been suggested that a better predictor of satisfaction may be the availability of opportunities—the availability of opportunities structured differently in different situations because of an individual's gender, age, rank or race (Schneider et al., 1992). Individuals of different gender, rank, age or race may be offered varying opportunities based on a judgement of the capability of a particular 'type' of person.

A person's ability is an individual variable that is correlated with job satisfaction. Schneider et al. (1982) found that the relationship between ability required for a job and job satisfaction, is as strong as the relationship between job rewards such as identity, autonomy and feedback, and satisfaction. Therefore, it is suggested that ability provides opportunity because the more one is capable of doing the more one has the opportunity to so do. Schneider et al. (1982) also suggested that there are individual differences in how important opportunity is to people. For example, the preference for intuition seems to be conducive to the pursuit of higher education and logically, a person who deeply values opportunity would also value education because of the options education provides. The field of individual differences and their effects on job satisfaction is an area of importance, but in need of further research to establish new theories on the nature of the relationships, or to provide more support for existing theories.

Comparative studies on the job satisfaction of other occupational groups, such as nurses, paramedics or university administrators, could usefully be undertaken in the future. Such studies could be aimed at identifying, not only the job satisfaction levels of these professionals, but also those areas where their job satisfaction levels are particularly high or low. These findings would be pointers for management who are morally entrusted to ensure that the levels of the job satisfaction of their workers are moderately high.

Several researchers have consulted the author about their intention to carry out job satisfaction studies in their organisations/countries. The results of such studies may later lead to a global theory of job satisfaction. Within UK higher education, a longitudinal study could be useful, to see if the level of job satisfaction found tallies with the findings in this book, or whether the job satisfaction level is rising or falling, and what the implications of such findings would suggest.

Finally a major area of further study is the relationship between job satisfaction and productivity. Are there any links, if so, what is the nature of such a relationship within the UK higher education sector? The author would be happy to hear from any researcher with research findings that build on results discussed in this book.

Appendix:
A copy of the questionnaire
used in the study

Dear Sir/Madam,

Several researchers have investigated the relationship between job satisfaction and certain variables. Most of the reported studies took place within industrial establishments. Using university teachers as subjects, this study attempts to investigate the relationships between age, gender, rank, length of service and job satisfaction.

Towards meeting these objectives, it would be appreciated if you will assist us by completing the attached questionnaire. All data collected from this survey will be treated as confidential and it will only be used for the purpose of this study.

A stamped and addressed envelope is enclosed for your convenience.

Yours faithfully,

THE RELATIONSHIP BETWEEN JOB SATISFACTION AND CERTAIN VARIABLES

##

Questionnaire Number

Questionnaire completed?

Y	N
1	2

≈≈≈

SECTION A

Please, circle the appropriate number of the answer or option that corresponds to your own situation.

1. Please, indicate your gender.

Male	Female
1	2

2. What is your rank or seniority?

Lecturer	Senior Lecturer	Reader	Professor	Other, please specify
1	2	3	4	5_____

3. For how many years have you worked in (a) your present university, (b) higher education?

Years	0–5	6–10	11–15	16–20	21–25	26–30	31–35	36+
(a)	1	2	3	4	5	6	7	8
(b)	1	2	3	4	5	6	7	8

4. What was your age on your last birthday?

Less than 25 years	25–34	35–44	45–54	55 years and over
1	2	3	4	5

5. In the following grouping, please indicate where your academic discipline belongs.

Medicine/Pharmacy/Dentistry	1
Engineering/Computing	2
Arts/Law	3
Natural Sciences/Agriculture	4
Social Sciences/Management	5
Other, please, specify _____	6

6. What is your leadership or management responsibility?

Head of Department or Division	1
Director of School	2
Dean of Faculty	3
Provost or Head of Unit e.g. an Institute	4
Not currently in charge of an academic unit or group	5
In charge of an academic unit/group not indicated above please, specify _____	6

≈≈

SECTION B

Please indicate, by circling the appropriate number in each case, the level of satisfaction or dissatisfaction which you derive from the following aspects of your job. Please, note that 1 on the scale represents "Extremely Dissatisfied", 4 represents "Indifferent" i.e. neither dissatisfied nor satisfied, and 7 represents "Extremely Satisfied".

	Extremely Dissatisfied	Very Dissatisfied	Dissatisfied	Indifferent	Satisfied	Very Satisfied	Extremely Satisfied
7. Teaching	1	2	3	4	5	6	7
8. Research	1	2	3	4	5	6	7
9. Your Administrative and Managerial Duties	1	2	3	4	5	6	7
10. Present Pay	1	2	3	4	5	6	7
11. Promotions	1	2	3	4	5	6	7
12. Head of Units' Supervision/Behaviour	1	2	3	4	5	6	7
13. Co-workers' Behaviour	1	2	3	4	5	6	7
14. Physical Conditions/Working Facilities	1	2	3	4	5	6	7

There are numerous specific factors, considerations, or aspects of your job which affect the level of your satisfaction or dissatisfaction. Examples of these include, the availability of funds for research, the size of the classes you teach, the criteria for promotion, the congeniality of your colleagues, the time available for research, the facilities for teaching, secretarial and clerical assistance, the amount of teaching, your future salary prospects, the equipment for research, the interest shown by the students, the manner in which your department head administers your department, your office facilities, your retirement benefits, the availability of technical assistance, et cetera.

15. Please, list five factors, considerations, or aspects of your job which contribute most to your dissatisfaction. Indicate the level of your dissatisfaction with each factor on a scale of 1 (Extremely Dissatisfied) to 3 (Dissatisfied).

	ED	VD	D
a.	1	2	3
b.	1	2	3
c.	1	2	3
d.	1	2	3
e.	1	2	3

16. Please, list five factors, considerations, or aspects of your job which contribute most to your satisfaction. Indicate the level of your satisfaction with each factor on a scale of 1 (Extremely Satisfied) to 3 (Satisfied).

	ED	VD	D
a.	1	2	3
b.	1	2	3
c.	1	2	3
d.	1	2	3
e.	1	2	3

SECTION C

17. Which one of the following indicates how much of the time you feel satisfied with your job:

1	Never
2	Seldom
3	About half of the time
4	Most of the time
5	All of the time

18. Which one of the following statements best describes how you feel about your job?

1	I hate it.
2	I dislike it.
3	I am indifferent to it.
4	I like it.
5	I love it.

19. Which one of the following statements describes how you feel about changing your current job?

1	I would quit this job at once if I could.
2	I would like to change my job soon.
3	I am not sure if I would exchange my present job for a similar one.
4	I am not eager to change my job, but I would do so if I could get a better job.
5	I would not exchange my job for any other.

20. Which one of the following statements best describes how you think you compare with other people?

1	No one dislikes his/her job more than I dislike mine.
2	I dislike my job more than most people dislike theirs.
3	I like my job about as well as most people like theirs.
4	I like my job better than most people like theirs.
5	No one likes his/her job better than I like mine.

Comments by the respondent:

Thank you for your co-operation in completing this questionnaire.

Bibliography

A

Abraham, K G and Medoff, J L (1984), 'Length of service and layoffs in union and non-union work groups', *Industrial and Labour Relations Review,* 38, 1, 87–97.

Abraham, K G and Medoff, J L (1985), 'Length of service and promotions in union and non-union work groups', *Industrial and Labour Relations Review*, 38, 3, 408–420.

Abu-Saad, I and Hendrix, V, (1995), 'Organisational climate and teachers' job satisfaction in a multi-cultural milieu: the case of the Bedouin Arab schools in Israel', *International Journal of Educational Development,* 15, 2, 141–153.

Adams, J S (1965), 'Injustice in social exchange' in L Berkowitz, (ed.), *Advances in Experimental Social Psychology,* 2, New York, Academic Press.

Adler, S and Golan, J (1981), 'Lateness as a withdrawal behaviour', *Journal of Applied Psychology,* 66, 544–554.

Aldag, R J and Brief, A P, (1975), 'Age and reactions to task characteristics', *Industrial Gerontology*, 2, 223–229.

Alderfer, C (1972), *Existence, Relatedness, and Growth: Human Needs in Organisational Settings*, New York, Free Press.

Anderberg, M J (1973), *Cluster analysis for applications*, Academic Press, New York.

Andrews, I R and Henry, M M (1963), 'Management attitudes toward pay', *Industrial Relations*, 3, 29-39.

Ariga, K, Brunello, G and Ohkusa, Y (1997), 'Promotions, skill formation and earnings growth in a corporate hierarchy', *Journal of the Japanese and international economies*, 11, 3, 347-384.

Association of Commonwealth Universities, (1993), *Commonwealth Universities Yearbook*, ACU, London, 3, 2170-2976.

Atchinson, T J and Lefferts, E A (1975), 'The prediction of turnover using Herzberg's job satisfaction technique', *Personnel Psychology*, 25, 53-64.

Audu, I (1972), 'The functions of a university' in Adaralegbe, A (ed.), *A Philosophy for Nigerian Education*, Heinemann Educational Books, Ibadan.

B

Bartol, K and Wortman, M (1975), 'Male versus female leaders: effects on perceived leader behaviour and satisfaction in a hospital', *Personnel Psychology*, 28, 533-547.

Bell, R C and Weaver, J R (1987), 'The dimensionality and scaling of job satisfaction: an internal validation of the Worker Opinion Survey', *Journal of Occupational Psychology*, 60, 147-155.

Black, B and DiNitto, D (1994), 'Volunteers who work with survivors of rape and battering: motivations, acceptance, satisfaction, length of service and gender differences', *Journal of Social Service Research*, 20, 1/2, 73-97.

Bone, A and Bourner, T (1998), 'Developing University Managers', *Higher Education Quarterly*, 52, 3, 283-299.

Bray, J H and Maxwell, S E (1985), 'Multivariate Analysis of Variance', *Sage University Papers Series on Quantitative Applications in the Social Sciences*, Sage Publications Ltd., London.

Brief, A P, Rose, G L and Aldag, R J (1977), 'Sex differences in preferences for job attributes revisited', *Journal of Applied Psychology*, 62, 5, 645-646.

Brockner, J and Kim, D H (1993), 'Factors affecting stayers' job satisfaction in response to a worker who departs for a better job', *Journal of Applied Social Psychology*, 23, 20, 1659-1684.

Brooke, P P, Russell, D W, and Price, J L (1988), 'Discriminant validation of measures of job satisfaction, job involvement and organisational commitment', *Journal of Applied Psychology*, 73, 2, 139-145.

Burke, R J (1966), 'Are Herzberg's motivators and hygienes unidimensional?', *Journal of Applied Psychology*, 50, 317-321.

C

Cameron, S (1973), 'Job satisfaction: the concept and its measurement', London, Work Research Unit, Department of Employment.

Carsten, J M and Spector, P E (1987), 'Unemployment, job satisfaction and employee turnover: a meta-analytic test of the Muchnisky Model', *Journal of Applied Psychology*, 72, 374-381.

Campbell, A, Converse, P and Rogers, W (1976), *The quality of American life*, New York, Russell Sage.

Centres, R and Bugental, D (1966), 'Intrinsic and extrinsic job motivations among different segments of the working population', *Journal of Applied Psychology*, 48, 88-92.

Church, J (ed.), (1994), 'Social Trends 24', *A Publication of the Government Statistical Service*, HMSO, London.

Church, J (ed.), (1995), 'Social Trends 25', *A publication of the Government Statistical Service,* HMSO, London.

Chia, Y (1995), 'The interaction effect of information asymmetry and decentralisation on managers' job satisfaction: a research note', *Human Relations*, 48, 6, 609-624.

Clark, A, Oswald, A, and Warr, P (1996), 'Is job satisfaction U-shaped in age?', *Journal of Occupational and Organisational Psychology*, 69, 57-81.

Clark, A E (1996), 'Job satisfaction in Britain', *Journal of Industrial Relations*, 32, 4, 189-217.

Clark, A E (1997), 'Job satisfaction and gender: why are women so happy at work?' *Labour Economics*, 4, 341-372.

Clayton, H R, Odera, V, Emenheiser, D A and Reynolds, J S (1998), 'The relationship of job satisfaction and family life: female managers in health care food service', *Marriage and Family Review*, 28, 1/2, 167-185.

Cranny, C J, Smith, P C, and Stone, E F (1992) *Job satisfaction: how people feel about their jobs and how it affects their performance,* Lexington Books, New York.

Cross, D (1973), 'The Worker Opinion Survey: a measure of shop-floor satisfaction', *Occupational Psychology*, 47, 193-208.

D

Dahl, T and Lewis, D R (1975), 'Random sampling device used in time management study', *Evaluation*, 2, 2, 20-22.

Davidson, M J and Burke, R J (eds.), (1994), *Women in Management: Current Research Issues*, Chapman Publishing, London.

Davies, G, (1994), 'Some Current Policy Issues in Higher Education', Conference Paper, *Conference of Queen's University and Schools,* 18th June.

DeSantis, V S and Durst S L (1996), 'Comparing Job Satisfaction Among Public and Private Sector Employees', *American Review of Public Administration*, 26, 3, 327-343.

Doering, M, Rhodes, S R and Schuster, M (1983), *The Ageing Workforce*, Sage Publications, Berverly Hills.

E

Eberts, R W and Stone, J A (1985), 'Male-female differences in promotions: EEO in public education', *Journal of Human Resources*, 20, 4, 504-521.

Edwards, A F (1979), 'Multiple Regression and Analysis of Variance and Covariance', San Francisco, W H Freeman.

Eggins, H (1994), 'Research priorities in higher education in the 1990s', Conference Paper, *Conference on research into higher education in the humanities*, Belfast, 23rd April.

Ejiogu, A M (1980), 'Theories of job satisfaction and job performance: an overview and critique', *Newland Papers*, Number Two, The University of Hull, Department of Adult Education.

Eichar, D M, Norland, S, Brady, E M, and Fortinsky, R H (1991), 'The job satisfaction of older workers', *Journal of Organisational Behaviour'*, 12, 609–620.

Etzioni, A. (1964), Modern Organisations, Englewood Cliffs, New Jersey, Prentice-Hall Inc.

Evans, L (1997), 'Understanding teacher morale and job satisfaction', *Teaching and Teacher Education,* 13, 8, 831–845.

Everitt, B (1974), *Cluster Analysis*, Heinemann Educational Books, London.

Everly, G S and Falcione, R L (1976), 'Perceived dimensions of job satisfaction for staff registered nurses', *Nursing Research*, 25, 3, 346–348.

F

Fairburn, J A and Malcomson, J M (1994), 'Rewarding performance by promotion to a different job', *European Economic Review*, 38, 683–690.

Fincham, R and Rhodes, P S (1999), *Principles of organisational behaviour*, Oxford University Press, London.

Finn, R H and Lee, S M (1972), 'Salary equity: Its determination, analysis, and correlates', *Journal of Applied Psychology*, 56, 283–292.

Flexner, A (1930), *Universities: American, English, German,* Oxford University Press, London.

Forgionne, G A and Peeters, V E (1982), 'Differences in job motivation and satisfaction among female and male managers', *Human Relations*, 35, 2, 101–118.

G

Gaertner, J F and Ruhe, J A (1983), 'Occupational stress in men and women accountants: is there a difference?' *The National Public Accountant*, 28, 38–42.

Ganzach, Y (1998), 'Intelligence and job satisfaction', *Academy of Management Journal*, 41 5, 526–539.

Gibson, J L and Klein, S M (1970), 'Employee attitudes as a function of age and length of service: a reconceptualisation', *Academy of Management Journal*, 13, 411–425.

Giles, W F and Feild, H S, (1978), 'The relationship of satisfaction questionnaire: item to item sensitivity', *Academy of Management Journal,* 21, 2, 295–301.

Goffee, R and Nicholson, N (1994), 'Career development in male and female managers—convergence or collapse?' in Davidson, M J and Burke, R J (eds.), *Women in Management: Current Research Issues*, Chapman Publishing, London, 80–92.

Glenn, N D, Taylor, R D and Weaver, C N (1977), 'Age and job satisfaction among males and females: a multivariate multistudy study', *Journal of Applied Psychology*, 62, 189–193.

Goh, C T, Koh, H C and Low, C K, (1991), 'Gender Effects on the Job Satisfaction of Accountants in Singapore', *Work and Stress,* 5, 4, 341–348.

Golembiewski, R (1977), 'Testing some stereotypes about the sexes in organisations: differential satisfaction with work?' *Human Resource Management,* 16, 30–32.

Gray, A M and Phillips, V L (1994), 'Turnover, age and length of service: a comparison of nurses and other staff in the National Health Service', *Journal of Advanced Nursing*, 19, 819–827.

Grimes, P W and Register, C A (1997), 'Career Publications and Academic Job Rank: Evidence from the class of 1968', *Journal of Economic Education*, 28, 1, 82-93.

Gruneberg, M M, Startup, R, and Tapfield, P, (1974a), 'The effect of geographical factors on the job satisfaction of university teachers', *Vocational Aspect of Education,* 26 63, 25-29.

Gruneberg, M M, Startup, R, and Tapfield, P, (1974b), 'A study of university teachers' satisfaction with promotion procedures', *Vocational Aspect of Education,* 26, 64, 53-57.

Gruneberg, M M and Startup, R, (1978), 'The job satisfaction of university teachers', *Vocational Aspect of Education,* 30, 76, 75-79.

Gruneberg, M M, (1979), *Understanding Job Satisfaction,* Macmillan Press Limited, London.

H

Hackett, R and Guion, R M (1985), 'A re-evaluation of the absenteeism-job satisfaction relationship', *Organisational behaviour and human decision processes*, 340-381.

Hackman, J R and Oldham, G R (1975), 'Development of the job diagnostic survey', *Journal of Applied Psychology*, 60, 159-70.

Halsey, A H and Trow, M A, (1971), *The British Academics,* Faber and Faber, London.

Hammer, W C and Smith F J (1978), 'Work attitudes as predictors of unionization activity', *Journal of Applied Psychology*, 63, 415-421.

Hanika, F deP (1963), 'How to study your executive day' in Copeman, G, Luijk, H and Hanika, F dep, *How the executive spends his time*, Business Publications Limited, London, 83-103.

Hanisch, D and Hulin, C L (1990), 'Job attitudes and organisational withdrawal behaviours', *Journal of Vocational Behaviour*, 37, 60-78.

Harrison, R (1961), 'Cumulative communality cluster analysis of workers' job attitudes', *Journal of Applied Psychology*, 45, 123-125.

Hersch, J and Viscusi, W K (1996), 'Gender differences in promotions and wages', *Industrial Relations*, 35, 4, 461-472.

Herzberg, F (1966), *Work and the Nature of Man*, Cleveland, World Publishing Co.

Herzberg, F (1968), One more time: how do you motivate employees?, *Harvard Business Review*, 46(1), 53-62.

Herzberg, F, Mausner, B and Snyderman, B (1959), *The motivation to work*, Wiley, New York, 2nd ed.

Hickson, C and Oshagbemi, T (1999), 'The effect of age on the satisfaction of academics with teaching and research', *International Journal of Social Economics*, 26, 4, 537-544.

Hinrichs, J R (1976), 'Where has all the time gone?' *Personnel*, 54, 44-49.

Holden, E W and Black, M M (1996), 'Psychologists in Medical Schools—Professional Issues for the Future: How are Rank and Tenure associated with Productivity and Satisfaction?', *Professional Psychology: Research and Practice*, 27, 4, 407-414.

Hoppock, J (1935), *Job satisfaction*, Harper and Row, New York.

Horne, J H and Lupton, T (1965), 'The work activities of 'middle' managers—an exploratory study', *Journal of Management Studies*, 2, 14-33.

House, R J and Wigdor, L A (1967), 'Herzberg's dual-factor theory of job satisfaction and motivation: a review of the evidence and a criticism', *Personnel Psychology*, 20, 4, 369-389.

Hui, C H and Yee, C (1999), 'The impact of psychological collectivism and workgroup atmosphere on Chinese employees' job satisfaction', Applied Psychology: an international review, 48, 2, 175-185.

Hulin, C L and Smith, P C (1964), 'Sex differences in job satisfaction', *Journal of Applied Psychology*, 48, 88-92.

Hulin, C L and Smith, P C (1965), 'A linear model of job satisfaction', *Journal of Applied Psychology*, 49, 209-216.

I

Imparato, N (1972), 'Relationship between Porter's Need Satisfaction: Questionnaire and the Job Descriptive Index', *Journal of Applied Psychology*, 56, 5, 397-405.

Iversen, G R and Norpoth, H (1987), 'Analysis of Variance', *Sage University Papers Series on Quantitative Applications in the Social Sciences*, Sage Publications Ltd., London.

J

Jacques, E (1961), *Equitable Payment*, New York: Wiley.

Joy, L (1998), 'Why are women under represented in public school administration'? *Economics of education review*, 17, 2, 193-204.

Judge, T A, Locke, E A, Durham, C C, & Kluger, A N (1998), Dispositional effects on job and life satisfaction: The role of core evaluations, *Journal of Applied Psychology*, 83(1), 17-34.

Jurgensen, C (1978), 'Job preferences: what makes a job good or bad?' *Journal of Applied Psychology*, 63, 267-276.

K

Kahn, R L (1960), 'Productivity and job satisfaction', *Personnel Psychology*, 13, 275-287.

Karp, H P, Nickson, J W and Jack, W (1973), 'Motivation hygiene deprivation as a predictor of job turnover', *Personnel Psychology*, 26, 377-384.

Katz, R and Maanen, J V (1976), 'The loci of work satisfaction' in Peter Warr (ed), *Personal goals and work design*, London, John Wiley and Sons.

Keith, P and Glass, L (1977), 'Sex differences in the perception of job factors', *College Student Journal*, 11, 43-48.

Killingsworth, M R and Reimers, C W (1983), 'Race, ranking, promotions and pay at a federal facility: a logit analysis', *Industrial and labour relations review*, 37, 1, 92-107.

King, N, (1970), 'Clarification and evaluation of the two-factor theory of job satisfaction', *Psychological Bulletin*, 74, 1, 18-31.

Kinman, G (1998), 'Pressure points: a survey into the causes and consequences of occupational stress in UK academic and related staff', *Association of University Teachers,* London.

Klein, S M and Maher, J R (1966), 'Education level and satisfaction with pay', *Personnel Psychology*, 19, 195-208.

Kong, B A, Chye, T G and Hian, C K (1993), 'The impact of age on the job satisfaction of accountants', *Personnel Review*, 22, 1, 31-39.

Konrad, A M and Cannings, K (1997), 'The effects of gender role congruence and statistical discrimination on managerial advancement', *Human Relations*, 50, 10, 1305-1328.

Kovach, K A (1993), 'Correlates of employee satisfaction with pay and benefits: public/private and union/non-union comparisons', *Journal of collective negotiations*, 22, 3, 253-256.

Kuhlen, R G (1963), 'Needs, perceived need satisfaction opportunities', *Journal of Applied Psychology*, 47, 56-64.

Kulik, C T, Oldham, G W, and Langer, P H, (1988), 'Measurement of job characteristics: comparison of the original and the revised job diagnostic survey', *Journal of Applied Psychology*, 73, 3, 462-466.

L

Lacy, F J and Sheehan, B A (1997), 'Job satisfaction among academic staff: an international perspective', *Higher Education*, 34, 3, 305-322.

Lam, S S K (1997), 'Job satisfaction among quality managers in Hong Kong: a survey', *International Journal of Management*, 14, 1, 103-106.

Larkin, J M (1990), 'Does gender affect internal auditors' performance?', *The Woman CPA*, 52, Spring, 20-24.

Lawler, E E and Porter, L W (1963), 'Perceptions regarding management compensation', *Industrial Relations*, October, 41-49.

Lawler, E E (1971), *Pay and organisational effectiveness: a psychological view*, New York, McGraw-Hill.

Lee, R and Wilbur, E (1985), 'Age, education, job tenure, salary, job characteristics, and job satisfaction: a multivariate analysis', *Human Relations*, 38, 781-791.

Lee, R T and Martin, J E (1996), 'When a gain comes at a price: pay attitudes after changing tier status', *Industrial Relations*, 35, 2, 218-226.

Lewis, G B (1986), 'Gender and promotions—promotion chances of white men and women in a federal white-collar employment', *The Journal of Human Resources*, 21, 3, 406-419.

Lewis, G B (1992), 'Men and women toward the top: backgrounds, careers and potential of federal middle managers', *Public Personnel Management*, 214, 473-491.

Lindsay, C A, Marks, E, and Gorlow, L (1967), 'The Herzberg theory: a critique and reformulation', *Journal of Applied Psychology*, 51, 330-339.

Lissmann, H and Gigerich, R (1990), 'A changed school and educational culture: job satisfaction and teacher satisfaction at *Gesamtschulen* in the state of Hessen, West Germany—some international comparisons', *Comparative Education*, 26, 277-281.

Locke, E A (1969), 'What is job satisfaction?', *Organisational behaviour and human performance*, 4, 309-336.

Locke, E A (1976), 'The nature and causes of job satisfaction' in M D Dunnette (ed.), *Handbook of industrial and organisational psychology*, 1297-1343, Chicago, Rand-McNally.

Locke, E A and Henne, D (1986), 'Work motivation theories' in Cooper, C L and Roberston, I (eds.) *International review of industrial and organisational psychology*. Wiley, London, 1-35.

Lofquist, L H and Dawis, R V (1969), *Adjustment to work—a psychological view of man's problems in a work-oriented society*, Appleton Century Crofts, New York.

Loher, B T, Noe, R A, Moeller, N L and Fitzerald, M P (1985), 'A meta-analysis of the relation of job characteristics to job satisfaction', *Journal of Applied Psychology*, 70, 2, 280-289.

Lorr, M (1983), *Cluster Analysis for Social Scientists*, Jossey-Bass Publishers, San Francisco, 7-8.

Luthans, F and Thomas, L T (1989), 'The relationship between age and job satisfaction: curvilinear results from an empirical study—a research note', *Personnel Review*, 18, 1, 23-26.

M

Mackay, L (1995a), 'The place of personnel in higher education', *Higher Education Quarterly*, 49, 3, 210-218.

Mackay, L (1995b), 'The personnel function in the universities of northern England', *Personnel Review*, 24, 7, 41-53.

Mahoney, T A (1979), *Compensation and reward perspectives*, Homewood (IL): Richard D. Irwin, Inc.

Malinowska-Tabaka, E (1987), 'Complex measures of job satisfaction\dissatisfaction among professionals', *Social Indicators Research*, 19, 451-473.

Marchese, M C and Delprino, R P (1998), 'Do supervisors and subordinates see eye-to-eye on job enrichment'?, *Journal of Business and Psychology*, 13, 2, 179-191.

Martinko, M J and Gardner, W L (1990), 'Structured observation of managerial work: a replication and synthesis', *Journal of Management Studies*, 27, 3, 329-357.

Maslow, A H (1954), *Motivation and Personality*, New York, Haper and Row.

Mason, E S (1995), 'Gender differences in job satisfaction', *The Journal of Social Psychology,* 135, 2, 143-151.

Mayfield, J R, Mayfield, M R and Kopf, J (1998), 'The effects of leader motivating language on subordinate performance and satisfaction', *Human Resource Management,* 37, 3 and 4, 235-248.

Mayo, E (1953), *The human problems of an industrial civilisation,* New York, Macmillan.

McClelland, D C (1967), *The Achieving Society,* New York, Free Press.

McGregor, D (1960), Theory X and Y, *The human side of the enterprise,* McGraw-Hill, New York.

McCarney, M, Edwards, S and Jones, R (1977), 'The influence of ethnolinguistic group membership, sex and position level on motivational orientation of Canadian Anglophone and Francophone employees', *Canadian Journal of Behavioural Science,* 9, 274-282.

Miles, E W, Patrick, S L, and King, W C (1996), 'Job level as a systemic variable in predicting the relationship between supervisory communication and job satisfaction', *Journal of Occupational and Organisational Psychology,* 69, 3, 277-292.

Misener, T R, Haddock, K S, Gleaton, J U and Ajamieh, A R A (1996), 'Toward an International Measure of Job Satisfaction', *Nursing Research,* 45, 2, 87-91.

Mobley, W H, Griffeth, R W, Hand, H H and Megino, B M (1979), 'Review and conceptual analysis of the employee turnover process', *Psychological Bulletin,* 86, 493-522.

Mottaz, C (1986), 'Gender differences in work satisfaction, work-related rewards and values, and the determinants of work satisfaction', *Human Relations,* 39, 4, 359-378.

Mottaz, C J (1987), 'Age and work satisfaction', *Work and Occupations*, 14, 3, August, 387–409.

Mueller, C W, and McCloskey, J C (1990), 'Nurses' job satisfaction: A proposed measure', *Nursing Research*, 39, 2, 113–117.

Murray, M A and Atkinson, T (1981), 'Gender differences in correlates of job satisfaction', *Canadian Journal of Behavioural Sciences*, 13, 44–52.

Mwamwenda, T S (1997), 'Teacher gender differences in job satisfaction in Transkei', *Research in Education*, 58, 1, 75–77.

N

Nathanson, I L and Eggleton, E (1993), 'Motivation versus programme effect on length of service: a study of four cohorts of ombudservice volunteers', *Journal of Gerontological Social Work*, 19, 3/4, 95–114.

Near, J P, Rice, R W and Hunt, R G (1978), 'Work and extra work correlates of life and job satisfaction', *Academy of Management Journal*, 21, 248–264.

Nicholson, E A and Miljus, R C (1972), 'Job satisfaction and turnover among liberal arts college professors', *Personnel Journal*, November, 51, 840–845.

Ninomiya, A and Okato, T (1990), 'A critical analysis of job-satisfied teachers in Japan', *Comparative Education*, 26, 249–257.

O

O'Brien, G E and Dowling, P (1981), 'Age and job satisfaction', *Australian Psychologist*, 16, 1, 49–61.

Olsen, D, Maple, S A and Stage, F K (1995), 'Woman and Minority Faculty Job Satisfaction', *Journal of Higher Education*, 66, 3, May/June, 267-293.

Orpen, C, (1995), 'The effects of perceived age-discrimination on employee job satisfaction, organisational commitment and job involvement', *Psychology*, 32, (3-4), 55-56.

Oshagbemi, T (1988), *Leadership and Management in Universities*, Walter de Gruyter, Berlin and New York

Oshagbemi, T (1995), 'Job Satisfaction of Workers in Higher Education', *Reflections on Higher Education*, 7, 8, 65-89.

Oshagbemi, T (1996), 'Job Satisfaction of UK Academics', *Educational Management and Administration*, 24, 4, 389-400.

Oshagbemi, T (1997a), 'Job Satisfaction Profiles of University Teachers', *Journal of Managerial Psychology*, 12, 1, 27-39.

Oshagbemi, T (1997b), 'The influence of rank on the job satisfaction of organisational members', *Journal of Managerial Psychology*, 12, 8, 511-519.

Oshagbemi, T (1997c), 'Job satisfaction and dissatisfaction in higher education', *Education + Training*, 39, 9, 354-359.

Oshagbemi, T (1998), 'The impact of age on the job satisfaction of university teachers', *Research in Education*, 59, 1, 95-108.

Oshagbemi, T (1999), *Managers and their Time*, Blackhall Publishing, Dublin.

Oshagbemi, T (1999a), 'Academics and their managers: a comparative study in job satisfaction', *Personnel Review*, 28, 1/2, 108-123.

Oshagbemi, T (1999b), 'Overall job satisfaction: how good are single versus multiple-item measures?', *Journal of Managerial Psychology,* 15, 5, 388-403.

Oshagbemi, T (2000a), 'Correlates of pay satisfaction in higher education', *International Journal of Educational Management*, 14, 1, 31-39.

Oshagbemi, T (2000b), 'Satisfaction with co-workers' behaviour', *Employee Relations,* 22, 1, 88-106.

Oshagbemi, T (2000c), 'Is length of service related to the level of job satisfaction?' *International Journal of Social Economics*, 27, 3, 213-226.

Oshagbemi, T (2000d), 'How satisfied are academics with their primary tasks of teaching, research and administration and management?' *International Journal of Sustainability in Higher Education*, 1, 2, 124-136.

Oshagbemi, T (2000e), 'Gender differences in the job satisfaction of university teachers', *Women in Management Review*, 15, 7, 331-343.

Oshagbemi, T (2001a), 'The time spent by academic managers on their primary tasks compared with the satisfaction derived from those tasks', *International Journal of Applied Human Resource Management,* 2, 1, 129-133.

Oshagbemi, T (2001b), 'Satisfaction of UK academics with their promotions', *International Journal of Applied Human Resource Management,* 2, 2, 49-63.

Oshagbemi, T (2001c), 'How satisfied are academics with the behaviour/supervision of their line managers?', *International Journal of Educational Management*, 15, 6, pp.283-291.

Oshagbemi, T and Hickson, C (2003a), 'Some aspects of overall job satisfaction: a binomial logit model', *Journal of Managerial Psychology*, 18, 4, 357-367.

Oshagbemi, T (2003c), 'Personal correlates of job satisfaction: empirical evidence from UK universities', *International Journal of Social Economics*, 30, 12, 1210-1232.

Oshagbemi, T and Ocholi, S (2013), 'Influences on leadership behaviour: a binomial logit model', *International Journal of Social Economics,* 40, 2, pp.102-115.

P

Palmore, E (1969), 'Predicting longevity: a follow-up controlling for age', *Gerontology*, (Winter).

Patchen, M (1961), *The choice of wage comparisons*, Englewood Cliffs, New Jersey, Prentice-Hall.

Paulin, E A and Mellor J M (1996), 'Gender, race and promotions within a private-sector firm', *Industrial Relations*, 35, 2, 276-295.

Pollard, G (1996), 'A comparison of measures of job satisfaction used in studies of social communicators', *Gazette,* 57, 111-119.

Porter, L W (1961), 'A study of perceived need satisfactions in bottom and middle management jobs', *Journal of Applied Psychology*, XLV, 1-10.

Porter, L W, Lawler, E E and Hackman, J R (1975), *Behaviour in organisations*, McGraw-Hill, New York.

Porters, L W and Steers, M (1973), 'Organisational work and personal factors in employee turnover and absenteeism', *Psychological Bulletin*, 80, 151-176.

Powell, G N and Butterfield, D A (1997), 'Effect of race on promotions to top management in a federal department', *Academy of Management Journal,* 40, 1, 112-128.

Q

Quarstein, V A, McAfee, R B and Glassman, M (1992), 'The Situational Occurrences Theory of Job Satisfaction', *Human Relations*, 45, 8, 859-873.

Quinn, R P, Staines, G L, and McCullough, M R (1974), 'Job Satisfaction: Is there a trend?', *Manpower Research Monograph No.30*, Washington DC, US Department of Labour, vi + 1-57.

R

Rhodes, S R (1983), 'Age-related Differences in Work Attitudes and Behaviour: A Review and Conceptual Analysis', *Psychological Bulletin*, 93, 328-367.

Richardson, A M and Burke, R J, (1991) 'Occupational Stress and Job Satisfaction among Canadian physicians', *Work and Stress*, 5, 4, 301-313.

Roberts, J A and Chonko, L B (1994), 'Sex differences in the effect of satisfaction with pay on sales force turnover', *Journal of Social Behaviour and Personality*, 9, 3, 507-516.

Robinson, S E, Roth, S L and Brown, L L (1993), 'Morale and job satisfaction among nurses: what can hospitals do?', *Journal of applied social psychology*, 23, 3, 244-251.

Ronen, S (1978), 'Job satisfaction and the neglected variable of job seniority', *Human Relations*, 31,4, 297-308.

Rosen, H and Weaver, C G (1960), 'Motivation in Management: a study of four management levels', *Journal of Applied Psychology*, XLIV, pp 386-392.

Roznowski, M (1989), 'Examination of the measurement properties of the JDI with experimental items', *Journal of Applied Psychology*, 74, 5, 805-814.

S

Sagie, A (1998), 'Employee absenteeism, organisational commitment and job satisfaction: another look', *Journal of Vocational Behaviour*, 52, VB971581, 156-171.

Scarpello, V and Campbell, J P, (1983), 'Job Satisfaction: Are the parts there?', *Personnel Psychology*, 36, 3, 577-600.

Schneider, B and Dachler, H P, (1978), 'A note on the stability of the Job Descriptive Index', *Journal of Applied Psychology*, 63, 5, 650-653.

Schneider, B, Reichers, A E and Mitchell, T M (1982), 'A note on some relationships between the aptitude requirements and reward attributes of tasks', *Academy of Management Journal*, 25, 561-574.

Schneider, B, Gunnarson, S K, and Wheeler, J K (1992), 'The role of opportunity in the conceptualisation and measurement of job satisfaction' in Cranny, C J, Smith P C and Stone, E F, (eds.) *Job satisfaction: How people feel about their jobs and how it affects their performance*, New York, Lexington, 53-68.

Schofield, P (1998), 'It's true: happy workers are more productive', *Works Management*, 51, 12, 33-35.

Schuler, R S (1975), 'Sex organisational level and outcome importance: where the differences are', *Personnel Psychology*, 28, 365-376.

Schwab, D P and Wallace, M J (1974), 'Correlates of employee satisfaction with pay', *Industrial Relations*, 13, 78-89.

Scott, K D and Taylor, G S (1985), 'An examination of conflicting findings on the relationship between job satisfaction and absenteeism: a meta-analysis', *Academy of Management Journal*, September, 599-612.

Senatra, P (1988), 'What are the sources and consequences of stress?' *The Woman CPA*. 50, 13-16.

Shapiro, J and Stern, L (1975), 'Job satisfaction: male and female, professional and non-professional workers', *Personnel Journal*, 54, 388-389.

Sheridan, J E, Slocum, J W and Buda, R (1997), 'Factors influencing the probability of employee promotions: a comparative analysis of human capital, organisation screening and gender/race discrimination theories', *Journal of Business Psychology,* 11, 3, 373-380.

Siassi, I, Crocetti, G and Spiro, H R (1975), 'Emotional health, life and job satisfaction in ageing workers', *Industrial Gerontology*, 2, 289-296.

Siu, O and Cooper, C L (1998), 'A study of occupational stress, job satisfaction and quitting intention in Hong Kong firms: the role of locus of control and organisational commitment', *Stress Medicine*, 14, 49-54.

Skinner, B F (1974), *About Behaviouralism*, Random House, Inc. New York.

Sloane, P and Williams, H (1996), 'Are 'Overpaid' Workers really unhappy? A Test of the Theory of Cognitive Dissonance', *Labour*, 10, 1, 3-15.

Smith, P C, Kendall, L M and Hulin, C L (1969), *The measurement of satisfaction in work and retirement: a strategy for the study of attitudes,* Chicago, Rand McNally.

Smith, P C, Kendall, L M and Hulin, C L (1975), *The Job Descriptive Index,* Bowling Green, Ohio, Psychology Department, Bowling Green State University.

Smith, P C, Kendall, L M and Hulin, C L (1985), *The Revised Job Descriptive Index,* Chicago, Rand McNally.

Smith, D B and Plant, W T (1982), 'Sex differences in the job satisfaction of university professors', *Journal of Applied Psychology*, 67, 2, 249-251.

Snell, S A and Baldwin, T T (1987), 'Promotions in the corporate world: comparing the perspectives of university professors, MBA students, and corporate managers', *Journal of Management*, 13, 3, 587-593.

Soutar, G N and Weaver, J R (1982), 'The measurement of shop-floor job satisfaction: The convergent and discriminant validity of the Worker Opinion Survey', *Journal of Occupational Psychology*, 55, 27-33.

Spinelli, M A and Gray, G R (1998), 'Employee satisfaction: are there differences among departments in the same hotel?', *Compensation and benefits management,* 14 4, 12-17.

Stagner, R (1975), 'Boredom on the assembly line: age and personality variables', *Industrial Gerontology*, 2, 23-44.

Staines, G L and Quinn, R P (1979), 'American workers evaluate the quality of their jobs', *Monthly Labour Review*, 102, 3-12.

Startup, R and Gruneberg, M M (1973), 'The academic as administrator and policy maker', *Higher Education Review,* 6, 1, 45-53.

Startup, R and Gruneberg, M M (1976), 'The rewards of research', *New Universities Quarterly,* Spring, 227-238.

Startup, R, Gruneberg, M M and Tapfield, P (1975), 'The satisfaction of university staff with their teaching', *Research in Education,* 13, May, 57-66.

Stewart, R (1984), 'The Nature of Management? A Problem for Management Education', *The Journal of Management Studies,* 21, 3, 323-330.

Stewart, R (1988), *'Managers and their jobs: a study of the similarities and differences in the ways managers spend their time'*, London, Macmillan, Second edition, 100-133.

Swimmer, G (1990), 'Gender based differences in promotions of clerical workers', *Journal of Industrial Relations*, 45, 2, 300-310.

T

Tamayo, A (1996), 'Value rankings and job satisfaction', *International Journal of Psychology,* 31, 3-4, 241-249.

Tang, T L, and Gilbert, P R (1995), 'Attitudes toward money as related to intrinsic and extrinsic job satisfaction, stress and work-related attitudes', *Personality and individual differences*, 19, 3, 327-332.

Taylor, F W (1947), *Scientific Management,* New York, Harper and Brothers.

Taylor, G S and Vest, M J (1992), 'Pay comparisons and pay satisfaction among public sector employees', *Public Personnel Management*, 21, 4, 445-454.

Thompson, D P, McNamara, J F, and Hoyle, J R (1997), 'Job Satisfaction in Educational Organisations: A Synthesis of Research Findings', *Educational Administration Quarterly*, 33, 1, 7-37.

Times Higher Education Supplement (1994), 'Sad life of the alienated academics'; 'UK scholars sing blues', 24 June, 1-2.

Times Higher Education Supplement (1998a), 'University female participation', 8 May p.5.

Times Higher Education Supplement (1998b), 'UK Outclassed in Pay League', 14 August, p.5.

Times Higher Education Supplement (1999a), 'Athena Project poised to raise profile of women in universities', 19 February, p.4.

Times Higher Education Supplement (1999b), 'Call to get tough on sex bias' 5 March, p.3.

Times Higher Education Supplement (1999c), 'Cambridge to recognise promotions', 28 May, p.6.

Times Higher Education Supplement (1999d), '9.2% of professors are women', 28 May, pp.20-21.

Times Higher Education Supplement (2000). 'Female/ethnic minorities league table'. 7 April, pp.18-19.

Toren, N (1993), 'The temporal dimension of gender inequality in academia', *Higher Education,* 25, 439-455.

Trowler, P (1997), 'Beyond the Robbins trap: re-conceptualising academic responses to change in higher education (or . . . Quiet Flows the Don?)', *Studies in Higher Education,* 22, 3, 301-318.

Truscot, B (1943), *Redbrick University,* Faber, London.

V

Verkuyten, M, Dejong, W, and Masson, C N, (1993), 'Job Satisfaction among Ethnic Minorities in the Netherlands', *Journal of Applied Psychology,* 42, 2, 171-189.

Vest, M J, Scott, K D and Masson, C N, (1994), 'Self-rated performance and pay satisfaction, merit increase satisfaction, and instrumentality beliefs in a merit pay environment, *Journal of Business Psychology,* 9, 2, 171–181.

Viswesvaran, C, Deshpande, S P and Joseph, J (1998), 'Job satisfaction as a function of top management support for ethical behaviour: a study of Indian managers', *Journal of Business Ethics*, 17, 4, 365–371.

Vroom, V H (1964), *Work and Motivation*, New York, Wiley.

W

Wahi, M C (1978), 'The job satisfaction theories: their applications and limitations', a paper presented for business administration 6304, *Organisational Administration*, Mankato State University, Mankato, Minnesota, USA.

Wanous, J P and Lawler III, E D, (1972), 'Measurement and meaning of job satisfaction', *Journal of Applied Psychology,* 56, 2, 95–105.

Wanous, J P, Reichers, A E and Hudy, M J (1997), 'Overall Job Satisfaction: How Good Are Single-Item Measures'?, *Journal of Applied Psychology*, 82, 2, 247–252.

Ward, M and Sloane, P (1998), 'Job satisfaction: the case of the Scottish academic profession', University of Aberdeen, mimeo.

Weaver, C N (1974), 'Correlates of job satisfaction: some evidence from the national surveys', *Academy of Management Journal,* 17, 373–375.

Weaver, C N (1977), 'Relationships among pay, race, sex, occupational prestige, supervision, work autonomy and job satisfaction in a national sample', *Personnel Psychology,* 30, 437–445.

Weaver, C N (1978), 'Sex differences in the determinants of job satisfaction', *Academy of Management Journal*, 21, 2, 265-274.

Weaver, C N (1998), 'Black-white differences in job satisfaction: evidence from 21 nation-wide surveys', *Psychological Reports*, 83, 1083-1088.

Weiss, D J, Dawis, R V, England, G W and Lofquist, L H (1967), *Manual for the Minnesota Satisfaction Questionnaire*, Minneapolis, Industrial Relations Centre, University of Minnesota.

Winstead, B A, Derlega, V J and Montgomery, M J and Pilkington, C (1995), 'The quality of friendships at work and job satisfaction', *Journal of Social and Personal Relationships*, 12, 2, 199-215.

Wishart, D (1982), *Cluster User Manual*, Inter University Research Council Series, Report No.47, (3rd Edition), 1978 and the Supplement to this Edition, April.

Wishart, D (1987), *Cluster analysis software*, Computing Laboratory, University of St. Andrews.

Witt, L A and Nye, L G (1992), 'Gender and the relationship between perceived fairness of pay or promotion and job satisfaction', *Journal of Applied Psychology*, 77, 6, 910-917.

Woodward, M (1983), 'On forecasting grade, age and length of service distributions in manpower systems', *Journal of the Royal Statistical Society Series A—Statistics in Society*, 146, 11, 74-84.

Wright, J D and Hamilton, R F (1978), 'Work satisfaction and age: some evidence for the job change hypothesis', *Social Forces*, 56, 4, 1140-1158.

Z

Zaleznik, A, Christensen, C R and Roethlisberger, F J (1958), 'The motivation, productivity and satisfaction of workers: a predictive study', Boston, Harvard University Graduate School of Business Administration.

Name Index

Subject Index

A three-way analysis of variance, 92, 109, 133, 145, 147, 152
A two-way analysis of variance, 120
Academic management/ managers, 17, 18, 31, 34, 36, 155
Academic workers, 116
Age-job satisfaction, 22, 94
ANOVA, 92, 98, 102, 105, 106, 109-111, 114, 115, 120, 122-125, 128, 133-135, 137
Association of university teachers, 131, 148, 152

Background of respondents, 17-18, 25, 26

Cluster analysis/ cluster analytical procedure, 63, 66, 73, 75, 77, 82
Commonwealth universities yearbook, 24
Concept of job satisfaction, 1, 3, 28
Consequences of job dissatisfaction, 1, 10
Cultural differences, 141

Definitions of job satisfaction, 1, 3, 4
Descriptive statistics, 98, 109, 120
Dispositional theory, 13

Employee attitudes, 2, 8
Equity theory, 36,
Existence, relatedness, and growth theory, 14
Expectancy theory, 14
Extrinsic/Intrinsic sources (of job satisfaction), 3
Intrinsic/Extrinsic rewards, 33, 96